# SONOROUS DESERT

Kim Haines-Eitzen

# SONOROUS

# DESERT

What Deep Listening

Taught Early Christian Monks—

and What It Can Teach Us

PRINCETON UNIVERSITY PRESS

PRINCETON AND OXFORD

Published by Princeton University Press
41 William Street, Princeton, New Jersey 08540
99 Banbury Road, Oxford OX2 6JX

press.princeton.edu

All Rights Reserved

First paperback printing, 2024
Paperback ISBN 9780691259284

The Library of Congress has cataloged the cloth edition as follows:

Names: Haines-Eitzen, Kim, author.
Title: Sonorous desert : what deep listening taught early Christian monks-and what it can teach us / Kim Haines-Eitzen.
Description: Princeton : Princeton University Press, [2022] | Includes bibliographical references and index.
Identifiers: LCCN 2021051264 (print) | LCCN 2021051265 (ebook) | ISBN 9780691232898 | ISBN 9780691237411 (ebook)
Subjects: LCSH: Listening—Religious aspects—Christianity. | Monastic and religious life—History—Early church, ca. 30–600. | Deserts—Religious aspects—Christianity. | Silence—Religious aspects—Christianity. | Solitude—Religious aspects—Christianity. | BISAC: RELIGION / Monasticism | RELIGION / Meditations
Classification: LCC BV4647.L56 H35 2022 (print) | LCC BV4647.L56  (ebook) | DDC 231.7—dc23/eng/20211130
LC record available at https://lccn.loc.gov/2021051264
LC ebook record available at https://lccn.loc.gov/2021051265

British Library Cataloging-in-Publication Data is available

Editorial: Fred Appel and James Collier
Production Editorial: Natalie Baan
Text Design: Carmina Alvarez
Cover Design: Katie Osborne
Production: Erin Suydam
Publicity: Kathryn Stevens and Maria Whelan
Copyeditor: Dana Henricks

Cover images: Saimoo Art / Adobe Stock; . / iStock

This book has been composed in Goudy Old Style

To John, Eli, and Ben,
who enrich my listening life
immeasurably

And to my parents,
who set me on a listening path
from the beginning

Listening is a primary mode
of understanding. As we listen to
the world around us, we come to
understand more deeply our
place within it. Our
listening animates the world. And
the world listens back.
—John Luther Adams,
*The Place Where You Go to Listen*

# Contents

Note to Readers and Listeners     xi

A Personal Prologue     xiii

1   **Listening to the Desert**     1

2   **Hermits and the Quest for Solitude**     23

3   **A Way of Silence in a Noisy World**     41

4   **Monastic Desert Soundscapes**     59

5   **Echoes in Sacred Canyons**     75

6   **Ascent at Sonorous Sinai**     93

7   **Finding Home in the Desert**     109

**Epilogue**     123

Acknowledgments     127

Desert Monasticism: A Brief Glossary     131

A Guide to Monastic Texts     133

Notes     137

List of Photographs     145

List of Recording Locations for Chapter Codas     145

# Note to Readers and Listeners

Accompanying this book are recordings I have made in desert environments. Sometimes these are recordings specific to a place; other times they are audio montages I've made from separate recordings to illustrate the themes I write about. The best way to listen to these recordings is to put on headphones. The desert is a subtle acoustic landscape and many of the quiet sounds will be lost without headphones. But more than that, I find that headphones can actually help us transport ourselves to another time and place, to close our eyes and imagine, to savor an experience of sound even if only for a few minutes. At the end of the book, I include information about where each of the recordings was made, including the segments of sound montages. The recordings themselves can be accessed by scanning or clicking on the QR code at the end of each chapter or by visiting https://press.princeton.edu/books/ebook/9780691237411/sonorous-desert.

I've also included a reading guide for monastic texts. The fact is that there was a rapidly growing literature about Christian monasticism beginning in the fourth century CE. In this book, I have drawn from the texts that speak most to the intersection of sound, desert, and monasticism, but they are only a small fraction of what is available. Although these texts were all written in languages other than English, I append a list of readily available English translations for those who wish to read the texts for themselves.

# A Personal Prologue

In the course of writing this book, I've been asked many times, usually by academic colleagues and friends, how I came to write about desert sounds and the ancient monastic quest for silence and solitude. They wonder how I, a historian of early Christianity and Judaism, could pivot from my earlier work on ancient scribes to a project about sound, hearing, and listening. The answer I have frequently given is that my work to this point has been focused on how the fact that most people couldn't read and write in the ancient world means we need to take sound and listening much more seriously in our understanding of the past. Most people in the ancient world heard the Bible, they didn't read it themselves; most people learned the stories of the ancient Greek and Roman gods by listening to stories or seeing them performed in the theatre, not by reading them. And the many ancient stories about the sounds of seduction (like the sirens who sing in Homer's *Odyssey*), the sounds of war (like the sounds of trumpets used to launch battles), and the sounds of the apocalypse (again, trumpets, but also peals of thunder and the sound of sheer silence) reveal just how much sounds inspired the ancient imagination. In a predominantly oral world, hearing and listening mattered.

But the truth is that my research into desert sounds and early Christian desert monasticism has been as much a personal journey as it has been an academic one. When I reflect now on that question—the question of how I turned toward themes of solitude, silence, nature, and the desert—I realize that in some ways I've been preparing to write this book my whole life. Seeds were sown in many places along the way.

None of us can remember the first sound we heard, for our ears and hearing develop while we are still in utero, beginning sometime around eighteen weeks. Six months before I was born, my mother fretted with my one-year-old sister inside our flat-roofed limestone home in the hills of Beit Jala, just to the south of Jerusalem, listening to the sounds of sirens and bombs in Jerusalem during the June war of 1967. My father had gone up the hill to watch from a rooftop as fighting unfolded.

My parents had moved to Jordan from Indiana the year before to study Arabic and to work with a humanitarian organization. They arrived full of hope and a commitment to service, instilled in them by their Mennonite backgrounds. Neither of them anticipated a war. I don't recall hearing the sounds my mother heard that June, of course, but I think somehow I learned something on a cellular level about sound and fear, place and identity, violence and belonging. I can only faintly imagine her fear, and the fear of so many women around the world, in a war-torn place. I began at an early age learning to listen, learning to keep quiet, learning to be watchful. A first seed, perhaps.

My mother likes to tell this story: when I was just a few months old, my parents drove from Beit Jala to Wadi Qilt, a historic canyon just east of Jerusalem, to visit the monastery of Saint George. She remembers how my father hiked up to the monastery, but she stayed in the cool shade at the base of the canyon, where the creek was flowing and the breeze moved through the trees, and I slept peacefully. So she says. I have returned to that monastery many times over the years, sometimes hiking the trails through the canyon. The research and writing of chapter 5 reminded me of my mother's story and enabled me to revisit a place I've known since infancy.

In subsequent years growing up in Nazareth on a hospital compound, where my father worked as a chaplain, we marked time by the call of the mosque's minaret five times a day, listened to the bells of the Basilica of Mary on Sundays, and knew where in town there were engagement parties or weddings, because the music resounded around the hills. We learned, too, the languages of Arabic and, later, Hebrew, adapting our ears and voices as needed. I listened closely to the doves and pigeons outside my window, knew when the gardener was working below by the sound of his reed flute, and, in 1973, heard the sirens that blared throughout the town during the Yom Kippur war. We listened to the sirens and took shelter in a cave dug into the limestone hill just across the road. It was quiet in there, the limestone flaking from the walls to the loamy floor. As a child, I thought it was somewhat festive, being interrupted from our dinner and needing to put our plates of food onto trays and walk across the street to the damp cave—a cave that also had an altar and chapel tapestries—to join friends from the compound. But this is, I'm sure, entirely too romantic a memory. The truth is sounds are often alarm calls and they can instill in us a visceral fear. We learn to keep safe by listening. And, sometimes, quiet is a comfort. The cool quiet of the forest behind the hospital compound, Kfar HaHoresh, was also a welcome respite from life (and death) at the hospital.

Each spring we used to load up our green Peugeot station wagon with a footlocker, carefully packed with cookware and food, strapped to the roof along with gallons of water, a tent, sleeping bags, and snorkeling gear, and set off for the Sinai desert. We would leave Nazareth long before sunrise and chart our progress with the rising sun as we traveled southward through the valley along the western side of the Jordan River. Our destination was usually the remote and mostly deserted slip of land on Dahab's shores of the Red

Sea. This was long before the days of five-star resorts and airport landing strips, well before any census-worthy residential communities beyond the nudist colonies and Bedouin settlements. The sounds of Dahab—the lapping of the Red Sea, the call of the Eurasian collared doves, and the clatter of pots and pans for cooking—were muffled by the sand and thatch shelters where we pitched our tent. The sound of the sea itself, where we spent long days snorkeling, had its own watery acoustic signature.

Sometimes our vehicle ran out of gas or got stuck in sand dunes; other times we were robbed in the middle of the night, but to me (and I think to the rest of my family), this was a desert paradise, rich with wildlife and history. However remote the location seemed, we knew we were not the first to set foot on these "wastelands." Biblical stories of the wandering Israelites had been emblazoned in our minds and imaginations; the evidence of medieval crusaders was visible in places like what is now called Pharaoh's Island. We understood that our route was profoundly historical. These trips to Sinai, as well as later treks on camels with friends in Sinai's interior and to Saint Catherine's monastery, had a long-lasting effect on my experience of landscape, history, and listening. And instilled in me a deep love of the desert.

During these same years, from the 1970s to the 1980s, we spent many Sunday afternoons at a small hermitage in Galilee. We would drive down from Nazareth through the valley headed eastward toward the village of Deir Hanna, a village named for the apostle John in the New Testament. Just beyond the village, we turned off into an olive grove, parked our car, and had a picnic. As kids we would climb the olive trees and search for tortoises. Then we made our ascent to the small monastery of Lavra Netofa. Founded in 1967 by two monks, one Belgian and one American, the hermitage was perched on a hilltop where a central building contained a kitchen and dining room, a small welcoming space where we sat on rug-covered mattresses to visit, and a few guest quarters. Small cabins were scattered on the hilltop to accommodate the monks' individual solitary sojourns. The monks carved a chapel in an ancient cistern located within the mountain itself—a cave chapel, reverberant and damp throughout the seasons of the year.

The rough road to the monastery was too difficult for our car, and I remember vividly what seemed like a long hike from the valley upward and around the last bend in the road to the very top of the mountain where the monastery's main building stood. Somehow the air up there was always cooler and there was a feeling of rest. Our arrival was met with the monks' welcome and hospitality, wild sage tea, and frequently an opportunity to enjoy the chapel. For me the wonder of the place lay in the goats feeding on sagebrush, the deep sense of calm, and the wonder of solitude. Above all, the quiet. Goats grazed, cats and their kittens played on the cement porches of the kitchen and dining hall, and monks' and visitors' voices were kept low, almost to whispers. The earthy scented air was dry and still.

I could not have understood in those days the nature of my own quest for solitude, but if I close my eyes now and recall Lavra Netofa, I am immediately transported to a time and place and experience, one that in many ways now no longer exists. The two founding monks, Fathers Yaakov and Toma, with whom we spent so many afternoons, have now passed away and the monastery is maintained by a small group of monks. When I last visited the monastery in 1996, the town of Hararit had been built right up to within a few footsteps of the chapel. There is no need to park at the bottom of the hill and hike up; there is little distance between the hermitage and the world. Solitude and community confront one another on a daily basis, each deferring to the other—just as they did in the past.

In writing these stories from my childhood, I find myself somewhat embarrassed by my own nostalgia, the rosy-colored glasses that tint my sense of the past. But the line between experience and reflection—between feeling and thinking—has never been straightforward or even a line at all. The experiences we have as children do shape the course of our lives. And, for me, they inspire the kinds of questions I ask in my research, the ways I am curious about how ancient people experienced place and belonging, and, most relevantly here, how hearing and listening—in deserts, in monasteries, in solitude—can reveal our deepest longing, fear, and sense of wonder. The past may haunt us, but it also propels and sustains us.

Finally, I fast forward to much more recent experiences that have, in some ways more directly, shaped this book. My ideas began to come into focus sometime around the year 2012. At the time, I was chair of my academic department, mother of two active young sons, and daughter to aging parents. I felt stretched. Home was a lively place of electric guitar, saxophone, viola, violin, cello; dogs and a cat and pet snakes (who didn't make much noise), fish, frogs and lizards (and the crickets needed to feed them), a cockatiel that whistled Mozart and chirped loudly for companionship; four goats (outside); and of course the cacophony of all of our voices, often overlapping in heated debate at mealtimes or over games. Campus was a nonstop stream of voices, needs, and requests. In the midst of such rich cacophonies, I craved silence and solitude.

As a family we also planned many daytrips and vacations oriented around our older son's avid interests in herpetology (the study of reptiles and amphibians), with the express aim of finding new species, especially snakes. We hiked local preserves looking for green, milk, and garter snakes. We quested for timber rattlesnakes throughout the Southern Tier of New York, where they are now protected. But we also traveled the country in pursuit of finding new species for our son's life list. And many of these trips were to the American Southwest. We spent summers traipsing through Utah, Arizona, and New Mexico on a mission to find as many different rattlesnake species as we could in the fewest number of days. The result? Nine rattlesnake species in nine days! Let me be clear: I love snakes and I love discovering and understanding the past. But one question kept troubling our son: Why did so many people recoil at the sight and sound of a snake? What made people so terrified of snakes that they would set bounties on them, round them up, slaughter them by the hundreds? In short, why are snakes vilified by so many?

These questions are ones that can be asked about the past as well as the present. And they led me to think more and more about how and why snakes are so frequently reviled in ancient Christian texts. In particular, I wanted to understand why demons in the stories of Christian desert monks were depicted as hissing like snakes. What was it about their *sound*, the particular sounds of a hiss, that terrified ancient monks? In many ways, my curiosity about this most particular of sounds—the sound of hissing serpents—was ignited by my son's passion for snakes and by our listening for the sounds of a snake's rattle. I began to record desert sounds, including the sounds of rattling snakes, like others might bring back a photograph from a family trip. Over time, these recordings became an essential part of my understanding of early Christian monasticism and I began taking trips on my own—to the American Southwest as well as to the Negev and Judean Deserts of my childhood—to see what I might uncover about how and why sound is such a powerful force in our lives.

The personal intimacies of family life braided themselves alongside my professional inquiry into the past. For me, the past has always been intertwined with the present: history shapes our contemporary world, our experiences today shape our understanding of the past. We dwell, I believe, in this dynamic relationship between the past and the present. So, too, I find that the stories from my childhood (and more recent ones) speak to the threads that tie place to practice: What we do and how we live is inextricably tied to where we are. Whether it is the practices of monasticism in the hills of Galilee or the remote Sinai Desert, the quest for solitude and silence in antiquity or today, or even the hunt for new species to add to a life list—these practices take place, well, *in* place. And coursing throughout these interconnected webs—personal and professional, past and present, practice and place—is a world of sound, if we only pause and learn to listen.

*Sonorous Desert* is my attempt to listen to the history of early Christian desert monasticism and to reckon with my own relationship to this history, to recognize that my own longings for quiet solitude, the sounds of nature in remote places, and the experience of belonging have been shared by others. We read to know we are not alone, C. S. Lewis may have once said, and I think we also research and write to reach across time and place, to join ourselves to others, to understand who we are in this world. Through listening we cross the threshold of time, place, and practice to embrace a rich and sonorous life.

# SONOROUS DESERT

# 1

# LISTENING TO
# THE DESERT

*The world is made of sound.*
—Tommy Orange, *There, There*

*Every soul has a distinct song.*
—Joy Harjo, *Crazy Brave*

Nearly 1800 years ago, a young Christian man, probably still a teenager, left his Egyptian village and journeyed in stages eastward beyond the shores of the Nile River and into the remotest desert wilderness. His name was Antony, and he sought a solitary, quiet, and undistracted life, which ultimately led him to become a hermit in a cave near the shores of the Red Sea. In the hands of his biographer, the bishop of Alexandria, Athanasius, Antony's quest was deeply thwarted: Antony faced crowds of people, who journeyed from far distances in the hopes of hearing his teachings. He also fought with cacophonous demons, who roared like lions, crashed like thunder, and hissed like snakes. Athanasius's sensational story of Antony lit the imagination and hearts of Christians throughout the Mediterranean world. In ever-greater numbers, Christians began taking pilgrimages to see Antony in the desert, many deciding to live as hermits themselves. Over time, from the late third century onward, monasteries were built to house groups of monks. Monasticism grew and flourished in the deserts of the Middle East between the third and seventh centuries. The desert became a sacred place— set apart as a place for contemplation, asceticism, and prayer. These developments changed the course of Christian history.

But there is an aspect to the story of Antony and those who followed him that has largely been forgotten: Antony left the noise and distractions of city life for the quiet of the desert, seeking solitude and silence and simplicity, but he found that the desert, too, was loud and distracting. The desert was surprisingly sonorous. He sought solitude, but community followed him. There is something quite reverberant about his story in our own world, where the incessant distractions of modern life and the ever-increasing noise of cities make many of us long for quiet solitude. In an effort to find quiet solitude, people are now drawn to YouTube "whispering" channels, take long solo treks on hiking trails, and go on meditation retreats. Antony's story is one of many from ancient Christianity that reveals timeless tensions between community and solitude, the pulls of family and work, and what it means to live a devoted life. Perhaps most relevant today is the way that his story wrestles with the paradox of noise and silence, especially the noise and silence of the desert, a place often described by absences—of people, water, animals, and sound. And here his story, as well as the stories of monks in the following centuries, speaks urgently to our own time. These stories reveal how monks became part of the natural history of the desert, how they were shaped by their experience of desert sounds, and how they in turn impacted desert soundscapes.

This is a book about how the sounds of the desert—sounds like wind, water, thunder, animals, and even humans—shaped the development of Christian monasticism in the Middle East. But it is also about what listening to the desert today can teach us about our own quest for quiet and stillness. It emerges from my belief that the past can teach us about the present, that our sounding world deeply shapes our sense of place and belonging, and that a religious movement—even the seemingly foreign practice of monasticism—can offer us new insight into our own changing world. Ancient Christian monks teach us about listening to the natural world, the quest for silence and solitude in arid lands, the paradoxical pulls of solitude and community, and the cultivation of deep inner quiet.

## Origins and Literatures of Early Christian Monasticism

Over the course of the first to fourth centuries CE, Christianity gradually spread in the towns and cities of the Roman Empire with an orientation toward community. The movement grew through communal connections—families, coworkers, neighbors—and it built institutional structures upon these relationships. Christians formed familial-like bonds, calling each other brothers and sisters. It was, and is, a deeply social religion. But from an early stage, Christianity, like Buddhism, also developed strong ascetic tendencies that eventually led to the vibrant, rich, and varied practices of monasticism that continue to this day. A variety of factors led to these developments, and a few key points are important to the themes of this book.

From its very origins, Christianity was inextricably tied to suffering: the story of a suffering Messiah, a Jesus crucified, and stories of his followers who were persecuted and martyred for their faith in him. But Christians also came to borrow from classical philosophy the ideals of self-control, concentration, and attention; and from Judaism, Christianity inherited the practices of fasting, prayer, and a reverence for sacred scripture. The word *asceticism*, which comes from the Greek word *askesis*, meaning "practice" or "training," refers to a wide variety of practices that Christians developed to withstand suffering in times of persecution, cultivate self-control, foster devoted and contemplative attention and inner quietude, and resist an attachment to worldly pleasures. Suffering came to be transformed into something to celebrate rather than to fear or avoid.

Monasticism grew from these ascetic tendencies. Our vocabulary here is both helpful and misleading. The term *monasticism* comes from the Greek word *monachos*, which meant "solitary one," but in fact monastic practices were remarkably diverse, especially in the early stages of the movement. There were some wealthy urban Christians who turned their homes into residential monastic communities for men or women who wanted to pursue a life of celibacy, prayer, and contemplation. Others, like Antony, sought to live as hermits, eking out an existence on the fringes of society or, even farther, in remote caves and canyons of the Middle East. For them, the primary goal seems to have been withdrawal and solitude. But in the late third and early fourth centuries (and beyond), monasteries gradually came to be built, sometimes with formidable boundary walls, to create spaces for communal monasticism. Still other forms blended the communal and the solitary: for example, monasteries were built adjacent or connected to a network of caves so that monks could have time for individual solitude in cave hermitages while also living as part of a community in the monastery itself. The diverse forms of early Christian monasticism may have contributed to its appeal. Over time, the variety of options for monastic living in locations throughout the regions of Egypt, Sinai, Palestine, and Syria coupled with the sensational stories of monks that circulated in oral and written form led to a flourishing of monasticism.

One place of monasticism, however, outshone nearly all others: the desert. The historian William Harmless notes in his book *Desert Christians* that "Egypt's deserts were the edge of the world, a vast and remote frontier land. Almost overnight, those deserts seized hold of the fourth-century imagination." But why did Christian monks choose the desert? After all, the deserts of Egypt, Palestine, and Sinai were regarded as uninhabitable wastelands—home to demons and the devil, dangerous wild animals, and marauding criminals. Why, then, did Christians, beginning in the third century, increasingly decide to become hermits and choose to live in monastic communities in the desert wastelands of the Middle East?

There is first the matter of simple geography and proximity: the Middle East is arid or semiarid. The distance between cities located in desert oases or along the Nile River and the surrounding desert wilderness was (and is) frequently very short. The threshold between community and solitude was narrow and easily traversed. Even today, aerial maps of Egypt illustrate this quite vividly: the narrow green line of cultivated fields and villages that runs north and south along the Nile River abruptly ends where the tan and brown desert escarpment, much of which is uninhabited, rises and extends to the east and west. The ancient walled city of Jerusalem offers another way to understand the distinctions between urban and rural, city and desert: just to the west and south of the ancient city, an ancient traveler would have quickly found themselves deep in the Judean and Negev Deserts. In antiquity, the distinction between town and desert, civilization and wilderness, was in many ways more stark than we find today.

There is an even more compelling reason why hermits chose to go into the desert, for by the time this movement began, the desert had a long religious history—as a place of danger and temptation, yes, but also as a place of wandering and revelation. The biblical stories of the ancient Israelites migrating through these deserts after they had been freed from slavery in Egypt were a key sacred narrative for early monks. So, too, were the stories from the New Testament Gospels of Jesus being tempted in the desert. In these stories and many others, the desert was an important place to go for solitude, to withdraw from society, to hear the voice of God. The practice of withdrawal—setting out on a journey, leaving one's home, going to a quieter place, and spending time alone—was both a biblical idea as well as a Greek and Roman one. Again, language may help us understand this ancient concept: the Greek word *anachoresis* meant withdrawal, retirement, retreat. It is from this ancient word that we get our English word *anchorite*, meaning "hermit." The idea of withdrawal was not new when Christianity began developing; it was already an old idea, one that existed long before Christianity emerged in the first and second centuries. In times of battle, it meant retreat to a safe place. But for philosophers, it meant something else. For the first-century Stoic philosopher Seneca, the idea of withdrawal was much more concrete: in one of his letters, he complains of the noise coming from the bathhouse below his writing studio. The noise becomes too much for him and he decides to withdraw to the country, a place that is more conducive to philosophy, concentration, and writing. A place decidedly quieter. Monks recognized this storied and sacred history of the Bible and drew upon philosophical ideas about the power of solitude as they made the desert their home.

Above all, the desert was a place of profound paradox that sparked the imagination: a place hot and cold, deathly dry but also home to violent floods, dangerous and yet potent with revelation and salvation, seemingly empty but with abundant evidence of humans and other animals, and surprisingly noisy and silent. It is in these paradoxes where we can best understand the cultivation of listening among ancient monks. And the monks' practices of meditation, concentration, and listening in the harsh desert environment, the image of the solitary hermit wrestling with the demons in the desert, and stories about the strength and resolve of these monks in the wilderness—these ideas traveled westward and eventually contributed to the establishment of Christian monasteries throughout Europe, the British Isles, and beyond. Reasons for choosing a monastic life naturally varied from person to person, and the geography, climate, and form of monasticism varied as well, but there was a common thread: a desire to "listen with the ear of the heart," as Benedict of Nursia, Italy, wrote in his influential sixth-century *Monastic Rule*.

Our information about early Christian desert monasticism comes from two main sources: a diverse collection of texts written in Greek, Coptic, Syriac, and Latin between the third and seventh centuries CE and recent archaeological excavations of ancient monasteries. Since the literatures of monasticism are diverse, it may be useful to orient the reader to the substantial written sources that reveal the history and development of desert Christian monasticism. Beginning in the late fourth century, we see the first biographies of individual monks written sometimes by their students or, if they were heads of monasteries, by their successors. Some of these biographies are full-length books, such as the *Life of Antony*; others are much shorter and found in collections of stories about monks in Egypt and Palestine. One such collection, the *Lausiac History*, was written in the fifth century by the writer Palladius. The most famous and widely distributed collection of stories and sayings of monks was called *Sayings of the Fathers*, an anthology that was written anonymously in the fifth or sixth centuries and circulated in two forms: one was organized alphabetically by the names of monks; the other was organized thematically. Other anthologies include the fifth century *History of the Monks in Egypt*, also written anonymously, and the late sixth- or early seventh-century book *The Spiritual Meadow*, written by a monk named John Moschos who traveled throughout the Middle East to collect and record the stories of monks. In addition to biographies and collections of stories and sayings, monastic rules for individual monasteries began to be written in the fourth century, with the most famous of these being the Pachomian Rule, which included guidelines for monks on nearly every aspect of daily life in the Pachomian monasteries, including details about how to observe daily prayers, maintain proper mealtime modesty and decorum, limit travel beyond the monastery walls, and contribute to the various tasks assigned to monks. Finally, there was a wide array of treatises, letters, and philosophical and practical instructions for monastic life that were written by monks beginning in the fourth century. I draw especially from one of these treatises in particular, *The Ladder of Divine Ascent*, written by the seventh-century abbot of Saint Catherine's monastery in Sinai, John Climacus. Whenever possible, I pair these texts with material evidence recovered from archaeological excavations, which are vital for understanding the complex and dynamic history of early Christian monasticism.

The literatures of monasticism, also sometimes called collectively the Desert Fathers, offer vivid windows into the history of monasticism. But even here we need to be cautious, because all of these texts were written in praise of individual monks, in praise of asceticism and monasticism. They aren't what we would consider "history" today. They are hagiographical texts—in other words, writings about the holiness of the Desert Fathers, the "saints." Still, they are essential to the story I tell in the coming chapters—a story about how the paradoxes of solitude and community, silence and noise, natural sounds that terrify and comfort, and a desert harsh yet sacred came to shape the development of Christian monasticism.

# Natural Soundscapes in
# a Time of Change

Our sounding world so deeply shapes our sense of place and our sense of who we are that we often forget to give sound the close attention it deserves. We live in a world of sound. Sounds encircle us, reverberate within our bodies, emanate from above and below. We are enveloped by the sounds of streets and traffic and labor, sounds of birds and trees and wind, of home and family and friends, of dissonance and violence, of voice and of silence. We swim in sound. And, in turn, we shape our acoustical environments and alter the workings of sonic biospheres. Sounds orient us in our world—they animate and enliven our sense of place, and entangle us in a reverberant ecology of place, time, and weather. Sounds guide us to food and safety, help us avoid danger and imminent destruction, and foster our sense of mystery, memory, longing, and belonging. They shift our gaze and change our behavior. Humans are not alone in the gravitational pulls of the sonorous; birds and trees and whales and many other beings are deeply shaped by their acoustic environments.

We do not need the physical ability to hear to be influenced by ambient environmental sounds. After all, sound is fundamentally a vibrational event—vibrations that have duration, frequency, and quality. Sounds vibrate and reverberate around us all the time. The well-known deaf percussionist, Evelyn Glennie, puts this most eloquently in her "Hearing Essay": "There is a common misconception that deaf people live in a world of silence. To understand the nature of deafness, first one has to understand the nature of hearing"; hearing, she claims, "is basically a specialized form of touch. Sound is simply vibrating air, which the ear picks up and converts to electrical signals, which are then interpreted by the brain. The sense of hearing is not the only sense that can do this, touch can do this too. If you are standing by the road and a large truck goes by, do you hear or feel the vibration?" Sounds are deeply tied to our sense of touch and our sense of well-being. In recent decades, we have learned especially about how important natural sounds are for our health, our connections to one another and to the environment, and our quality of life.

"We are," naturalist and acoustician Michael Stocker writes in *Hear Where We Are*, "always submerged in sound and vibration; it excites our ears and touches our bodies, our skin and our bones." We feel sound and it shapes the places we work, where and how we live, and how we travel. It also shapes a sense of who we are—we hear *where* we are, we hear *who* we are. Sounds trigger memories and animate our daily narratives. Phenomenology can help us understand how essential soundscapes are to our experience of life itself. As a philosophy of lived experience, phenomenology teaches us that the body is fundamental to perception and sensation, as David Abram articulates in his book *The Spell of the Sensuous*. He writes that "the body is that mysterious and multifaceted phenomenon that seems always to accompany one's awareness"— an idea that is important for understanding how sound shapes our sense of place and who we are in a place. How we experience the sounds around us is interwoven with our collective and individual identities, and paying attention to sound offers us an opportunity to come into our bodies, inhabit our place of being, and understand who we are.

Tuning into sounding worlds is now more urgent than ever, because climate change is altering natural soundscapes in dramatic ways. UNESCO called 2020 the "Year of Sound," in part because our natural soundscapes are changing so rapidly. Much of what is unfolding in real time today was predicted almost sixty years ago by Rachel Carson in her book *Silent Spring*: "Over increasingly large areas of the United

States," she wrote, "spring now comes unheralded by the return of the birds, and the early mornings are strangely silent where once they were filled with the beauty of bird song. This sudden silencing of the song of the birds, this obliteration of the color and beauty and interest they lend to our world have come about swiftly, insidiously, and unnoticed by those whose communities are as yet unaffected." Audubon and Cornell University's Lab of Ornithology released reports in the spring of 2020 indicating that some 30 percent of the birds around the world have been lost since 1970. So, too, scientists have shown a dramatic collapse in insect populations. Even the sonic dimensions to marine life have changed, including the decline of whale populations and the silencing of their sonority because of the dramatic increase in the noise of shipping traffic.

New water patterns affect sound, too. The loss of waterways—due to drought, for example, and to draining and redirecting rivers and creeks for use in agriculture—contributes to both a silencing of natural sound as well as the desertification of landscapes. Marc Reisner's *Cadillac Desert* traces the history of how the American West's water has been lost and the devastating effects of dams, overuse, and agriculture. "We set out to tame the rivers," he writes, "and ended up killing them." The fact is that deserts around the world are growing in size and "dry places," as William deBuys writes in his book about the American Southwest *A Great Aridness*, will become "drier." Reduced water means fewer birds and fewer animals more generally. In the polar regions, where ice is melting more rapidly than ever, the acoustical changes go in the opposite direction as the calving of icebergs and sound of waterfalls occur in new places with dramatic sonorous effects.

Wildfires, too, have an enormous impact on the sound of the environment—both in the noise they produce and the silences that lie in their wake. In Norman Maclean's poetic telling, the noise of a crown fire sounds "like a train coming too fast around a curve and may get so high-keyed the crew cannot understand what their foreman is trying to do to save them." A deafening noise leading to utter silence. In 2020, Australia experienced one of the most devastating bushfire seasons in its history. We do not yet know what the full impact will be of fire on wildlife, but it is likely to change the natural soundscape for a long time to come. The same is true of the American West where fire seasons appear to be lengthening and intensifying, forever changing the environmental soundscapes of the region.

The changes in our natural soundscapes are compounded by the simultaneous amplification of human-generated (anthropogenic) sounds: the sounds of jets, trucks and cars, sounds of urbanization and development and industry. It is increasingly difficult to experience our natural world without the intrusion of such sounds. In the late 1960s, just as the composer R. Murray Schafer was beginning to conceive of his World Soundscape Project with the goal of attending to the increasing problem of noise, the environmental movement began to grow and flourish in North America. Environmental writers like Edward Abbey, ranger for Arches National Park in the 1960s, was an early proponent of protecting the national parks from anthropogenic noise. And the National Park Service's extensive ongoing research into noise pollution in the national parks shows just how deleterious the effect of human noise on wildlife can be, with the most striking example of noise pollution being the problem of tourist helicopter flights over the Grand Canyon National Park. And noise isn't just a problem in national parks; how challenging it is to find quiet in our everyday places of home and work, too.

In response to the environmental movements of the late 1960s, the historian Lynn White Jr. wrote an article called "The Historical Roots of Our Ecological Crisis," in which he argued that the problem of ecological change and environmental degradation was due to the "triumph" of Christianity over paganism in the ancient world. He claimed that "Christianity is the most anthropocentric religion the world has seen" and that Christianity rejected ancient animistic ideas about how God or gods or spirits could be found in natural objects like wood, trees, streams, mountains, and so forth. Instead, White argued that the Christian version of creation, found in the biblical book of Genesis, where God gives Adam power to name animals and power over the natural world, fostered a sense of nature as a resource solely for human consumption. White's arguments have been highly influential, and his essay is often cited in books and articles about environmental degradation and climate change. While there are some important ideas in his essay, my research on how monks were shaped by environmental sounds and how they regarded sounds as important signs—signals of safety or signals of danger—suggests an interdependence between monks and the natural world that cautions us against White's simplistic argument. One of the best ways to see the mutual dependence between monks and their desert environments is through the monastic sayings and stories about desert soundscapes. It is time, I believe, to rethink White's claims and to uncover a more nuanced history.

The sayings and anecdotes of the monks in the deserts reveal an interdependence between humans and other animals, between humans and their environment. This relationship between monks and animals, between monks and the desert, manifests itself in monastic stories about desert soundscapes. The sounds of crashing thunder, wind whistling through reeds, the howls of wolves and hisses of snakes—these and many other sounds taught monks lessons about listening and about living in relationship. Monastic literatures suggest that the sounding environment shaped monks' sense of both where they were and who they were. At times, the sounds signaled danger, such as the arrival of armies and impending war; at other times, sounds signaled safety, such as the sound of water in a parched landscape. And, as we see today, the development of monasticism in the desert also led to a reshaping of those soundscapes—the sound of the semantron, the wooden board that was used to call monks to prayers, was just one example of the anthropogenic changes monks brought to the landscape.

The ancient Christian monks who left their villages and cities for the quiet of the desert knew what we are increasingly recognizing today: the sounds around us shape our sense of place, of who we are, and our feelings of belonging and our feelings of alienation. I am interested in the ways that monks wrestled with the external sounds of the world, how they cultivated a quality of inner listening, and what we might learn about our own world from their experience and their stories. How in the midst of cacophonous surroundings might we cultivate a sense of inner quietude? How might we protect the places that provide us with the solace of bird song, wind, waves, and so many other natural sounds as our world thrums ever more noisy? These questions are at the heart of my inquiry into the past. For me, the desert—paradoxically both noisy and silent—is a compelling place to reconsider our care for the environment. And the first step is to listen.

## Acoustic Paradox of the Desert

Imagine a single sound. The sound of nothing, of emptiness— the sound of silence. Listen and imagine more closely and perceptively: perhaps you hear a slight ringing in your ears, the sigh of your breath, or the beating of your heart. Listen yet again and soft sounds emerge from the silence—a slight gust of wind, a distant bird, an echo of rock faint and nearly imperceptible. You are seated along the rim of a vast landscape of sand dunes, rock, and craggy mountains. All around you are the telltale colors of desert—the scorched and bleached earth, rusty and tawny. Below lies a wide-open valley floor with the distinctive snaking outline of an ephemeral river, a desert wadi now completely dry. You begin to feel the noonday heat, you close your eyes to the bright sun, and again you hear nothing. You are alone and the landscape seems utterly devoid of life—an empty wasteland.

The silence you hear is a sound experienced by desert dwellers and travelers for thousands of years. The dramatic landscape of the desert, vast and formidable, contrasts with its primordial silence. Cast a wide net and you will find many throughout history have described the desert as stark and silent. One has only to recall the stage for the biblical prophet Elijah's revelation, which is set in the wilderness after a sound of "sheer silence." Eucherius, a fifth-century bishop in Lyon, France, wrote that "no sound is heard in the desert save the voice of God." Modern travelers to the desert have similarly noted the silence. T. E. Lawrence, the famed Lawrence of Arabia, remarked on both the "friendly silence of the desert" and the "silence" that tormented his ears in the Arabian Desert—a deafening silence. And John C. Van Dyke, the American art historian turned desert lover in the early twentieth century, praised the deserts of the Southwest for their quiet: "The desert is overwhelmingly silent. . . . But . . . for all the silence, you know that there is a struggle for life, a war for place, going on day by day." Countless have sought the desert wilderness for a quiet that makes possible revelation. It is a land designed for hermits and solitaries, nomads and restless adventurers. If there is an acoustical signature associated with the desert—real and imagined—surely it must be its overwhelming silence.

But there is another perspective on the acoustical desert, long evoked by some of the very same visitors and residents. Travel down into that valley floor and you will find an oasis with clear water, a waterfall cascading over rocks, trees and brushy reeds rustling with a cool and shaded breeze, and pigeons with their guttural warble. Listen again. Here the desert is overwhelmingly sonorous and resonant. Stay awhile, until the wind picks up, and you may hear an echo of biblical proportions. In Moses's final song to the Israelites before he ascends Mount Nebo and to his death, he rehearses how God brought the Israelites through a "desert land," in a "howling wilderness." C. Leonard Woolley and T. E. Lawrence's survey of the Zin wilderness in the southern Negev and northern Sinai Deserts reported that the "the noise of the falling water . . . is so great that a man cannot hear himself speak."

The sense of "howling wastelands" reverberates in striking ways in seventeenth- and eighteenth-century Puritan narratives about conquest of the Americas, where fear and ambition collided. Explorations of the American Southwest by John Wesley Powell and others likewise noted the "perpetual roar" of desert canyons. Pause to imagine these sounds: the wind as it "howls" around and through desert caves and canyons, the excess of spring floods, rolls of thunder across barren escarpments, and even, if you allow yourself to imagine with the monks of late antiquity, the sounds of demons hissing and cackling in the dark. You might encounter here at the water's edge people in conversation, cattle and horses, machines and industry—all driven by the availability of water. Listen again and you might hear the sounds of military ranges, strategically placed in "empty" deserts, and the sounds of vibrant city life. The desert grows cities.

The striking acoustical paradox of the noisy and silent desert, the cacophony of its lively cities and the quiet emptiness in remote reaches, pulls at our imaginations. To those who have lived in the desert their whole lives, who have inherited traditions from their ancestors who also lived there, the variety of sounds, the desert's multilingual voices, are often experienced intuitively. For those less familiar, it may seem strange that a landscape or environment most often associated with desolation and absence—one that superficially, at least, may appear dead—could invite careful listening. But from the soft sounds of wind through a juniper to the crash of thunder, the desert is surprisingly sonorous and rich with sound if we pay attention.

The fact is that the desert has never been deserted and the signs of human, animal, and plant life in the desert extend for thousands of years. Prehistoric rock art, native and indigenous traditions, and the material histories of desert life all speak to the powerful ways that the desert is alive with sound. The most vital resource in the desert is, of course, water. Geographer Nick Middleton offers the following definition of a desert: "an arid zone . . . where the supply of water by all forms of precipitation is exceeded by the water lost via evaporation and transpiration." In such dry places, humans have resided in the "microhabitats" where water can be found in the desert: oases, springs, ephemeral streams, rivers—all of these water sources have supported human life. These habitats also nourish plant life and provide for animals and birds; they are rich with sonority, and their ecology includes the coexistence of humans and animals. Humans have impacted desert regions even as they are also affected by them—a relational history that is ever evolving.

## Learning to Listen by Recording

In the spring of 2015, I was seated at the canyon rim of the Zin wilderness, a place of storied traditions about Moses and the Israelites in Israel's Negev Desert. I was trying to capture the sound of desert silence that made such an impression on monks and travelers over the long course of history with a set of microphones and a digital recorder. My research had already begun on desert sounds and the development of Christian monasticism, but I had become frustrated by my reliance on ancient texts. I wanted to *experience* the acoustical desert. And, above all, I wanted to understand what it might mean to peel back the layers of history and to hear the faintest echo of the sounding past. I had hoped for silence or, at least, some quiet natural sounds free of anthropogenic noise. But I found myself frustrated at every turn by the intrusion of distant trucks, ubiquitous air traffic, dogs barking, and the whistling starlings flitting about the canyon walls. Slowly and reluctantly, I gave way to the experience of elusive silence, noting that this too was an important feature of monasticism—the desire for solitude, stillness, and quiet was always sought but seldom found. I also became convinced that the quest for silence, and claims of a silent desert, often came at a price—namely, the silence of those who had long inhabited these lands.

Since 2012, I have been making field recordings in desert environments. As I intimated in the prologue, I began to record the sounds of nature while on vacations with my family when my children were young. I suppose my first impulse was to capture a sound that we had heard just like we might capture a moment on camera—a memento to remind us of our trip. These recordings were like souvenirs from our travels. In this sense, my early attempts to capture sounds resonate with Susan Stewart's remarks in her 1993 book *On Longing*:

"The souvenir speaks to a context of origin through a language of longing, for it is not an object arising out of need or use value; it is an object arising out of the necessarily insatiable demands of nostalgia." Listening to these early recordings now returns me to a different time and place. Hearing, memory, nostalgia, and longing are closely intertwined.

But over time, I began to hone my skills in recording nature, because I became convinced that listening to the desert today might teach us about the acoustic desert of the past. The practice of recording the desert also became a practice of listening. I enrolled in Cornell University's Lab of Ornithology's Natural Soundscape Recording Workshop in 2013. The workshop that year was based in the Sierra Nevada mountains at San Francisco University's Field Campus and the instructors were experienced field recordists, experts in radio production, and ornithologists. Most of the students were advanced graduate students and avid birders who wanted to use recordings of particular birds and other animals to understand animal communication, behavior, and ecology. I was there to understand how field recording might enable me to better understand early Christianity monasticism.

Equipped with a set of microphones mounted on a tripod, a digital recorder slung crossbody and attached to headphones, I began to travel on my own—to the four North American deserts and to the deserts of southern Israel—becoming increasingly convinced that the practice of recording, as well as the content of my recordings, could teach me something about ancient monasticism. At first, my goal was to have an experience of being completely alone in the desert: to sit on my folding camp stool and listen closely to the sounds around me while capturing them on my recorder. I would try to find the most remote possible location—a place where there would be no human noise, no cars and trucks, no jets, and no voices. I wanted to be both awed and afraid. Could

I imagine myself into the deserts of late antiquity? Could I imagine what ancient monks experienced? We can't know, of course, about past experiences, but history writing does require imagination. And, I think, experimentation. And here language can help, for the closest word we have for "experience" in ancient Latin is *experimentia*: to experiment also meant to experience. Field recording was and is for me both experimental and experiential.

Recording also taught me to listen. I didn't leave microphones set up for hours and do something else, I sat and listened through the headphones to the sounds of the place. The field recordist Peter Cusack has written that "if you're a field recordist then you get to listen very intently to where you are recording; that develops your listening all the time. . . . If you get into an intense listening mode you can actually hear a huge amount, not just sounds, but the spaces between them and their relativity, the acoustics of the place." This resonates with my own experience. Field recording is an exercise in deep listening and it requires time: find a good location, set up the equipment, pause, quiet my own body, turn on the recorder, and just listen. And frequently the microphones—high-quality omni microphones—captured sounds my own ears couldn't hear: the voices of hushed campers in a remote area of Big Bend National Park; the sounds of footsteps in the oasis Ein Aqev in Israel's Negev Desert; distant military practice in the Zin wilderness. Field recording is both contemplative and frustrating. In our world, even the most remote-seeming desert places are teeming with anthropogenic sound.

In this sense, there is an important reverberation of the ancient monastic quest for silence and solitude—one that they found always deferred, always frustrated. Listening and recording provide discoveries about the contemporary world but also about the past. Some of the sounds I've captured in my recordings are sounds that I had completely missed in reading monastic texts—the croak of a raven, the silence in midday desert heat, the sound of rocks clattering down a cliff. There is a kind of conversation that can speak across time and medium (text and recording), one that reveals something about our own world and our place in it. It's important to emphasize that the recordings that now accompany this book are not intended to teach readers and listeners exactly what ancient monks heard, but rather to provide an evocative register and moments of listening that take us beyond the written word. The word *evoke*, which comes from the Latin word that meant "to call forth," is fitting here, as my goal in sharing recordings from desert environments is my own attempt to call forth a reverberant past, to cultivate wonder and imagination, and to illustrate how the past might speak to our present through sound.

Ancient monks inhabited a surprisingly and richly sonorous desert, a place chosen for its challenges and potent paradoxes. In doing so, they transformed the desert from a feared landscape into a sacred and desirable one. The call of the desert was also a call of the ear and the heart. And by understanding their call, we can nurture our own practices of listening.

## CODA

The desert's rich sonority—its quiet and its noise—can sometimes be experienced over the course of a single night as winds go from gentle and calm to loud and blustery. And then there are the springs, perhaps at dawn, where birds begin their song beneath rustling palm trees. Move into the canyon and arrive at a waterfall cascading down a limestone cliff. There the pigeons warble alongside white-winged doves. Heat rises, winds still, the workday begins: jets fly overhead, traffic on roadways picks up, and sheep and goats are corralled in metal holding pens.

# 2
# HERMITS AND THE QUEST FOR SOLITUDE

*What draws us into the desert is the search for
something intimate in the remote.*
—Edward Abbey, *A Voice Crying in the Wilderness*

*There is no possible return if you have gone deep
into the desert.*
—Edmond Jabès, *Intimations The Desert*

Early one morning in November of 2016, I was seated on a slip of sand at the entrance to the Santa Elena Canyon in Big Bend National Park recording the sounds of a contested river—the Rio Grande, running the border of Mexico and Texas. In all directions, the vast Chihuahuan Desert landscape with towering mountains and ocotillo, prickly pear, and sage-scrub lowlands arrayed itself in the dawn light. I was completely alone. Talk of drug smugglers and a border wall was in the air that fall, and as I faced the sheer, massive limestone cliffs before me, one stateside and one Mexican, I wondered where a wall could be built. With my recording gear and stool, I sat for a long time listening to a river that sounded like what the poet Jim Harrison called "the creek that actually burbles." All was calm, quiet, and although I had heard ravens as I drove towards the canyon, here even the birds were mostly silent. An occasional rustle of desert willow and cottonwood trees at the water's edge and the rippling water reverberated against the canyon walls. I was acutely aware of being alone on the border, this territory that had been so vilified in the news. I listened for footsteps. In solitude, fears do creep in quickly.

Before long, border patrol and park service propeller planes were flying overhead, even as birds began to chirp and flit about. The wind picked up. And then a tour bus arrived, leaving its motors running while tourists spilled out wide-eyed into the dramatic landscape. A chainsaw began its maintenance just down the river. The stillness and potency of aloneness evaporated quickly. The solace and fear I'd been feeling moments earlier gave way to irritation, and I packed up my equipment and moved on.

Two days earlier, I had spent a couple of nights in Comstock, Texas, at an RV park owned by a former border patrol agent named Allan Wright. I was hoping to record the sounds of Seminole Canyon and the Rio Grande and Pecos Rivers—places with famed petroglyphs in caves along canyon cliffs. On this particular recording trip, I was interested in making desert recordings in caves with rock art, having become curious about the ways in which pictographs, so ubiquitous in deserts around the world, might provide a visual dimension to the sonic landscape. A colleague of mine, the herpetologist Harry Greene, had suggested that I take a look at Seminole Canyon; there, in a cave, was an image of a wild cat, mouth wide open with lines coming out. Some had interpreted the lines as the "soul," he said, but I wondered if they couldn't depict the sound of the cat's scream. I also wanted to get down onto the rivers to record the sounds of water, birds, and frogs and to record sounds from within Parida and Panther Caves, located along the Rio Grande and only accessible by boat. These famed caves contain some of the most exquisite polychromatic rock art of the Southwest: complex murals of animals and humans painted with earth colors by hunters and gatherers of this region thousands of years ago.

Wright introduced me to a couple from Marfa, Texas—Edie and Gary—who were staying at the park with their pontoon boat. They said they could take me up the rivers the next morning. Over margaritas and rum and cokes, we talked about the border wall, about what the pictographs meant, and about the religious imagination, which Wright said was his thing when I told him I was writing about how desert sounds have shaped religious experience. I set out with Edie and Gary very early the next morning for the drive to the boat launch on the Pecos River. Low winds, serene rivers, a sunrise glinting against the canyon walls, and bitter cold—not unusual conditions for November. My field notes from that morning recount the songs of canyon wrens, ravens, swallows, frogs, and the pitiful cries of goat kids clambering with their mothers along impossibly sheer canyon walls. These sounds, along with our own voices, the trucks driving along Route 90 that stretches east and west, and, in late morning, a train passing overhead across the Pecos River, were captured in my recordings. Usually, I like to be alone for field recording because I hope to experience and record natural sounds free from any human sound. But that morning, I was glad for Edie and Gary's company. They knew how to listen. And how to wonder at these borderlands.

Every time I make field recordings, I discover something new. On this particular trip to the southern border of Texas, I wrestled with solitude and community. I hiked alone in Seminole Canyon, savoring solitude; I sought solitude at

Santa Elena canyon and found it only briefly. Solitude was a solace, but it was also discomforting. Encountering others was comforting and frustrating. But these pulls—between solitude and community—encouraged me to look more closely at the early history of monasticism.

To understand how monasticism might be rooted in precisely this paradox—a desire for solitude and a dependence on community—the place to begin is with hermits. There is a central tension in the stories of ancient hermits that resonates with my own experience of field recording: how they craved solitude, sought it in the deserts of ancient Egypt, Palestine, and Sinai, and how frequently their efforts to find it were thwarted. Time and again, community propelled them toward solitude; solitude returned them to community. In this sense, their quest was not dissimilar to the tensions that many now experience, caught between the pulls of solitude and community. The monastic literatures speak to an ambivalence about solitude: the quest for solitude inspired many to undertake a monastic life, but community was essential and inextricably linked to life in the desert.

## The Story of Antony

We begin with a closer look at the story of Antony, as told by Athanasius, the fourth-century bishop of Alexandria, Egypt. The overarching narrative of the *Life of Antony* is simple: Antony was a young Egyptian Christian, possibly from the village of ancient Koma (modern Qiman al-Arias, on the western shore of the Nile River south of Cairo), who longed from childhood to be "unaffected by the outside world." His parents died sometime in the last half of the third century, when he was a teenager, and he was left to care for his young sister. Scripture, in the telling of Athanasius, was important for young Antony. Burdened by the care of his younger sister, he was reminded one day on the way to church of the disciples who gave up everything they owned to follow Jesus. Inspired, Antony left the church and sold or gave away all of his belongings, keeping just a little to support his sister. Sometime later, again in church, he heard the Gospel passage "Do not be concerned about tomorrow," and he decided to leave his home, eventually his village, and move farther and farther out into the desert to free himself from the distractions and burdens of his family and village life, leaving his sister in the care of nuns. In Athanasius's story, Antony's journey began with a moment of hearing and listening, paying attention to the words in his head and the voice reading scripture.

Over the course of the long narrative, Athanasius recounts a sequence of departures: Antony's withdrawal from his house to the area outside of his house, his subsequent departure to a location outside of his village, then a departure to the "outer desert," and finally his departure to the "inner desert"—what would have been considered the farthest edge of the eastern Egyptian desert, close to the Red Sea. The plotline depends on this movement, this migration from town to remote desert. While we do not know for certain the historical details of Antony's life, Athanasius tells a dramatic and instructive story of this important anchorite, a term that now comes to take on religious significance: to be an anchorite, to be a hermit, meant giving up everything for a life of solitude and spiritual devotion, to depart from civilization for the remote wilds. Here, in a lonely place, the hermit might find an intimate encounter with the divine.

Central to the story of Antony is a specific place, a landscape—the desert, both imagined and real. The Greek word that Athanasius uses for desert, *eremos*, was a common word at the time. In Greek, this could refer to a deserted place, a wilderness, a desert, but it could also refer to a person's state of aloneness or being in solitude. In other words, a single word was used both for a place and a person, the desert and the hermit, the person who lives alone. Our English word *hermit* has its roots precisely in this multivalent Greek term. The desert lent itself well to the pursuit of solitude: as an extreme landscape, the desert, as Belden Lane has suggested in his book *The Solace of Fierce Landscapes*, "helps in forcing a breakthrough to something beyond all previously conceived limits of being." Life on the edge of what is possible—the story of Antony speaks to fragility and strength, spiritual devotion and the constant threat of imminent destruction. In this sense, the desert offered hermits the potent paradox of safety and danger.

But given Antony's quest for solitude and his withdrawal from society to seek it in the desert, one of the most striking features of his story is how little solitude he found even in remote "wastelands." He withdrew to find solitude, but solitude became elusive. In the first stage of Antony's withdrawal from society, he establishes himself outside "in front of his house," because, as Athanasius says, "no monk at all knew the remote desert"—at least, not yet. Gradually, he moves toward places outside his village. From another ascetic, another monk, he learns about living a solitary life and about ascetic discipline, the practices of prayer, manual labor, and meditation on scripture. Antony's *anachoresis* is a practice embedded in a sense of place.

We have little archaeological evidence to show what the lives of the earliest hermits were like, but in Athanasius's telling, Antony's journey is not a peaceful one: he is tormented by the devil and demons. Because the devil and demons play such an important role in the story of Anthony, it is worth pausing for a moment to unpack the cultural and historical context of the story briefly. Life for the vast majority of the inhabitants of ancient Egypt, and the ancient Mediterranean world more broadly, was precarious and fragile. Women frequently died young in childbirth; children died of disease, starvation, or abandonment; life-spans were short. In the ancient world, there was also a widespread view that God, or a multiplicity of gods and demons, as well as other supernatural beings, had powers to influence one's life. To ensure that things might go well for you, that you would have safe travels, a good harvest, strong health, you needed to worship the right gods in the right ways. Likewise, when you were afflicted with illness, your child died, or drought claimed your crops, it could indicate that you had not performed the right rituals for the right gods and you were being punished. In this context, the devil and demons were seen as adversaries that had the ability to interfere in your life negatively. And the desert was their home. Historian David Brakke writes that "the Christian monk was formed in part through imagining him in conflict with the demon, which in turn gained its identity through its relations to its monastic opponent." Demons foil Antony's quest for solitude, and also his search for silence.

The next stage of Antony's withdrawal takes place at some tombs at some distance from his village. There the devil beats him "with so many blows that he was left lying on the ground, unable to speak because of the torturous blows." The desert becomes a cacophony, filled with the sounds of demons. Consider the following passage, which appears early in the narrative just after Antony has made a break from the city to the desert. At the tombs one night, the demons made such a racket (*ktupon*) that that whole place seemed to be shaken apart. . . . Suddenly, the place was filled with the illusory shapes of lions, bears, leopards, bulls, and poisonous snakes and scorpions and wolves, and each of them was moving about in ways appropriate to its own form. The lion was roaring, wanting to leap on him; the bull acted as though it would gore him; the snake crawled forward but did not reach him; the wolf rushed at him, but then stopped. Absolutely terrible were the cacophonous ravings of all these apparitions and the howling of their voices.

The language here would have had rich resonance for ancient readers: the term *ktupon* was the word used for the sound of crashing thunder, the rattling of chariots or pounding of horses' hooves, the sounds of many voices raised up at once or the sounds of mourners beating their breasts. It is also onomatopoeic: when said aloud *ktupon* sounds like the objects it represents. In fact, much of the language that Athanasius uses to describe the sounds Antony hears is onomatopoeic: at various points in the narrative he hears hissing (*surittousin*); roaring (*brukhe*); cacophonies (*kakophone*).

But there is another way to read the passage. Note the variety of sounds that are represented in Antony's tomb hermitage: earth sounds, like the sounds of thunder; animal sounds, such as a roaring lion; and then the howling of voices. The sounds inform Antony's sense of where he is and who he is—he is in the place of demons, engaged in a fight against them, and trying to maintain his ascetic practice. His hermitage at the tombs was not Henry David Thoreau's idyllic Walden. Antony was not alone, and he did not find quiet.

After he is assaulted by the sounds in the tombs, Antony sets out for a mountain farther in the desert, eventually finding deserted military barracks. There he sets up a new hermitage in the ruins, which Athanasius describes as infested with reptiles. By now, however, the story of Antony and his resolve to keep pushing toward ever more solitary places in the desert had begun to spread throughout Egypt and beyond. Pilgrims came to see Antony in the desert, to listen to his battle with the demons: visitors heard, Athanasius writes, "what sounded like mobs of people creating a ruckus and a crashing around inside, letting loose their pitiful voices and crying out, 'Get away from what belongs to us! What are you doing in the desert?'" The demons here continue to attack Antony and claim that the desert is their own, as if to reaffirm the ancient idea that the desert is home only to demons.

According to Athanasius, Antony spent some twenty years at these barracks, and his fame spread widely throughout this period. Many chose to follow his example, so much so that Athanasius says, "The desert was made a city by monks." Antony began to teach those who came to see him; above all he taught them about the demons, how they first attack with thoughts, then with apparitions, and then by speaking loudly—an ever-increasing acoustic disturbance. Then, Antony said, they chant psalms, imitate the monks, and tell lies: "Frequently, without becoming visible, they pretend to chant with sacred songs, and they recite sayings from the Scriptures. And even when we are reading they are able to say right away and repeatedly, as if in echo, the same things we have read. While we are sleeping they arouse us for prayers, and they do this incessantly, hardly allowing us to sleep." Finally, their frustration leads them to become even noisier: "They do all these things—they talk and create uproars and play-act and stir up trouble—in order to lead astray those who are sound. What is more, they make obnoxious noises and clap their hands and laugh maniacally and hiss. But if no one pays attention to them, from then on they weep and wail because they have been defeated." The paradoxes of solitude in the desert now made communal ("a city"), and the silent desert now made noisy, are key to the sensational story Athanasius tells. These paradoxes create a tension in the narrative, but they also point to something deeper.

One of the subtle points of Antony's story is about listening. Athanasius encourages his readers to ask themselves: What sounds should be given attention and which ones should be ignored? How do the sounds Antony encounters shape a sense of who he is? These questions are intimately tied to a practice of solitude, where the inner and outer acoustic worlds become, I think, more audible. We can hear our own thoughts more clearly when we are alone, and that is one of the reasons so many poets and artists have written eloquently about the value of solitude. Antony's story is as much about his inner thoughts—the way the demons come to him through distracting thoughts—as it is about outer sounds—the demons who tempt, taunt, and torture him day and night and the mobs of pilgrims clamoring for his attention. Was Antony's struggle, at least in part, about developing a practice of deep listening? Of learning to pay attention? For anthropologists who study the relationship between music and trance, "imagination becomes experience" in the context of trance experiences. Was Antony caught up in the whirling tension of solitude and community, and silence and noise? If so, then his story offers insights into finding balance between these extremes.

## Anchorites and Cenobites

Antony was not the only Christian hermit in the fourth century. A few years after Athanasius wrote the *Life of Antony*, the Bible scholar, interpreter, and translator Jerome wrote the story of Paul, whom he calls "the first hermit." Paul, like Antony, "fled to the mountain wilds" and took up a life of solitude. As far as we can tell, the hermitage where Paul spent his life was just across the South Galala Plateau, a mountain range near the Red Sea in Egypt's eastern desert, from Antony's hermitage. In the Judean Desert of Palestine and along the Jordan River, hermits also began to settle in the fourth century. Men and women, it seems, were drawn to the anchoritic life, the life of solitude. In the fifth century, we learn about Sabas, who lived in solitude in Wadi Kidron, just to the southeast of Jerusalem and east of Bethlehem. The story of Sabas, written in the sixth century, says that Sabas had a vision in which an angel told him to go to a cave in the gorge and to "make it your home."

We don't have exact numbers for how many attempted to follow the example of these hermits. Some of our texts suggest there were many who became hermits, but the archaeological remains of such individuals is quite meager. We also cannot know for sure from this distance in time whether Antony, Paul, or Sabas actually lived in the caves that tradition attributes to them. What we do know is this: hermits attracted pilgrims and visitors, in some cases so much so that over time monasteries were built at the site of or near to the hermit's cave or shelter.

Cenobitic monasticism stands only partly in contrast to anchoritic. The term *cenobite* comes from another Greek word: *koinobios*, which meant "a communal life"—to live in community. The cenobitic form of monasticism became, over the course of centuries, the most common: a monastery, sometimes surrounded by walls, where groups of monks or nuns were housed together; a religious community that shared a daily liturgical schedule of prayer and work; a community where monks worked collectively to support the needs of the monastery.

Beginning in the fourth century, Christian monasteries came to be built throughout Egypt, Palestine, Sinai, and Syria. Monastic rules were also written to regulate the lives of those living in these communal settings. Everything from daily routines to noise at mealtimes, laughter, and sleep habits came to be regulated. Many of the stories and sayings we have of monks, as well as the monastic rules, reveal the tension between solitude—even imagined solitude—and the realities of communal life.

There is a frequent phrase, with some variations, that appears in the *Sayings of the Desert Fathers*: "Go and stay in your cell; your cell will teach you everything"; "Stay seated in your cell"; "Just sit in your cell." These "cells" were sometimes small, individual rooms in the monastery. They were also sometimes caves in the canyons just outside the monastery. Whatever the place, the sacred space, these sayings urged monks to seek solitude. In his 1996 book *Hermits: The Insights of Solitude*, Peter France has suggested that "solitude was not merely an escape from distractions; it was a teaching presence." But this quest for solitude in the midst of community, the life of being alone together, also raises questions: What does it mean to seek solitude in community? To seek the deserted place in a city? Can one have a life both in solitude and in community? These are questions raised by the ancient monastic texts. And they are questions that continue to resonate today.

The Monastery of Saint Antony along the Red Sea in Egypt, built in the fourth century soon after Antony's death and at the site associated with his hermitage in the remote desert, was one of the earliest monasteries. And it continues to operate today. So, too, the monasteries of Saint Paul in Egypt, Saint Sabas southeast of Jerusalem, and many others continue to house practicing monks. Cenobitic monasticism's paradox of solitude and community explains, in part, why it has flourished throughout history. To withdraw so as to find solitude in community offered a blend of the extremes of isolation and crowds. The cadences of desert monasteries tuned monks' attention to the present moment, to their spiritual practice, and to the ambience of place. The documentary film *The Last Anchorite* tells the story of a modern monk, Father Lazarus, who journeyed from Australia to the monastery of Saint Antony in Egypt in order to be free from distractions and live with "undisturbed attention." He speaks of the "lonely way" as a "rich spiritual way." There are lessons here for those of us who lead deeply social and embedded lives about what it means to cultivate solitary attention.

## Modern Quests for Solitude

Early Christian hermits sought solitude in the wilderness. But today, the quest for solitude is not restricted to religious hermits. Even as loneliness is now seen as an epidemic that has negative health impacts, the search for solitude is alive and well. Solitude and loneliness are not the same thing. Vision quests, meditation retreats in remote locations, solo through-hikes on wilderness trails—these are experiences for which we now expend tremendous funds, time, and energy. We seem to long for the undistracted life, for a sojourn in reclusive quiet that allows a slowed sense of time and the presence of attention. Although we often think of hermits as counterculture oddities, many people seek something of their isolation.

Writers, poets, artists, and modern-day monks have long recognized the potent possibilities for creativity that solitude affords and cultivates. Virginia Woolf offered an extended meditation on the writer's need for solitude in her 1929 book *A Room of One's Own*. Poets like May Sarton, who wrote the line "alone one is never lonely," and William Wordsworth, who praised "the bliss of solitude"—these sentiments seem to resonate in our own quests for solitude. Perhaps some of this can be attributed to a "rugged individualism," an admiration for the idyllic image of Thoreau, or the gnarled and edgy solitude of Edward Abbey, who ranted against paved roads in America's national parks in the 1960s (it would bring too many visitors, he said, and those visitors would only appreciate the wilderness from the window of a car). Thomas Merton, perhaps the most well-known twentieth-century hermit-monk, wrote in his book on solitude and freedom: "Why do I live alone? I don't know. . . . I cannot have enough of the hours of silence when nothing happens. When the clouds go by. When the trees say nothing. When the birds sing. I am completely addicted to the realization that just being there is enough."

But how do we now balance the pulls for solitude and community? We are at once confronted by a yearning for fewer distractions on the one hand, and our love and need for family, friends, community on the other. The romanticized idea of living as a hermit would come with tremendous loss. That is the paradox we live in today's busy and fast-paced world. But I wonder if we might embrace the push and pull of solitude and community—to find a kind of balance, an equilibrium that allows us to rethink our ideas about time and attention. The monastic literatures offer us one route toward balance.

In the summer of 2019, I visited Saint Anthony's Greek Orthodox Monastery in the Sonoran Desert south of Phoenix, Arizona. The August day was hot and the monsoon rains had not yet arrived, although the clouds looked promising that day. I wore a long skirt, long sleeves, and wrapped my head in a wool scarf to observe the modest dress requirements for visitors. The long, pine tree–lined road to the monastery was unmistakably desert: sandy soil, mesquite and cactus flats, dry and increasingly desolate. But the monastery itself, perhaps one of the most recent monasteries built in honor of Saint Antony, is a garden now. The most prominent sounds of the place that day were wind through pine and cypress and palm trees, the white-winged doves cooing, and above all, the sounds of water from the many fountains.

After being greeted at the gatehouse and bookstore, I walked the circuit of chapels and fountains, from Saint Anthony's church to the chapels of Saints Nicholas, George, Demetrios, and Seraphim. The chapels with their exquisite woodwork and painted icons were impressive, and their interiors were cool. Places to rest. I found a sense of solitude, in spite of workers, monks, and visitors throughout the grounds. But what was most striking to me was the sound of water—the fountains create a soundscape somewhat dissonant to the dry landscape—and they brought me back to the swish and burble of the sandy Rio Grande River. Water, so precious and ephemeral in desert landscapes, seems an especially apt metaphor for thinking about solitude.

Here again, a poet joins ancient monks to guide us. Wallace Stevens's poem "The Place of the Solitaires" speaks precisely to the relationship between water and solitude:

Let the place of the solitaires
Be a place of perpetual undulation.

Whether it be in mid-sea
On the dark, green water-wheel,
Or on the beaches,
There must be no cessation
Of motion, or of the noise of motion,
The renewal of noise
And manifold continuation;

And, most, of the motion of thought
And its restless iteration,

In the place of the solitaires,
Which is to be a place of perpetual undulation.

Stevens may have been writing about the poet's life, but the language he uses reverberates with the expressive sentiments of ancient monks: solitude is not static. To be alone in one's cell, one's cave hermitage, is not to stagnate in an unchanging and passive experience of life. Solitude is an opportunity to confront the undulations, the flow of movement both internal and external. It is also an opportunity to listen to the sometimes-subtle shifts happening within ourselves and in our ambient world. And to be returned, again, to community by way of listening. In this sense, the quest for solitude brings home the vitality of another paradox: silence and noise.

## CODA

 What does desert solitude sound like? Is it the experience of sitting alone at a borderland river before massive cliffs listening to a single bird? Or perhaps hearing your own footsteps as you move through the desert scrub only to come upon a mockingbird singing his repertoire? Solitude in the desert is frequently eerie: wind howls through nut trees in the ruins of an old ranch, the wind-pump creaks as it draws water, a catbird squawks an alarm. In the end, you are alone with the wind and the birds at dusk as darkness descends.

# 3

# A WAY OF SILENCE IN A NOISY WORLD

*Instead of raw or achieved silence, one finds various
moves in the direction of an ever-receding horizon
of silence—moves which, by definition, can't ever
be fully consummated.*
—Susan Sontag, "Aesthetics of Silence"

June is not the best time of year to visit Death Valley National Park. Located within the Mojave Desert of southern California, the park wears its hottest-place-on-earth reputation proudly. With temperatures averaging 110 or more degrees each day, many of the campgrounds are closed during the summer months and the visitor guide recommends enjoying locations "from your vehicle." But my goal was to get out into the desert, to record the sounds of Death Valley, to listen for signature sounds—sounds that might be distinctive or unique to the place. I was also hoping for silence. The park's maps describe Death Valley like this: "So empty, so vast, so simple, so quiet." That sounded enticing.

Three days earlier, I had flown into Las Vegas, Nevada, to meet with Ashley Pipkin, a resource specialist with the Natural Sound and Night Skies division of the National Park Service, which "works to protect, maintain, and restore acoustical and dark night sky environments throughout the National Park System." She invited me to spend a day with her monitoring the acoustic effects of a new highway near Lake Mead. We scrambled out early with her intern to check microphones and replace batteries in the recorders she had placed above the new highway and to note the amount of road and air traffic with an app designed by the National Park Service for this purpose. Sitting quietly for thirty minutes or more, we logged the various sounds we heard: jets overhead, powered hang gliders, trucks along the highway, occasional birds. The National Park Service was interested in documenting how the new highway's noise might change the behavior of wildlife, especially birds, and perhaps permanently alter the natural soundscape. Much of what we heard that morning was the sound of air traffic—a nearly constant stream of jets, helicopters, and prop planes. The highway, not fully completed, emitted little road noise beyond construction trucks.

After learning about Pipkin's work, I set out for Death Valley, on my way to a natural sound recording workshop scheduled for mid-June in the Sierra Nevada mountains. I stopped in at Ash Meadows National Wildlife Refuge, an oasis in the Mojave Desert, where the wind was blowing so hard through willows and desert scrublands that I struggled to set up my recording equipment at the impossibly turquoise Crystal Reservoir. Each gust thumped at my ears and microphones alike. The reeds at the water's edge bent sideways in great undulating waves. Heat was intensifying as I headed to Beatty, Nevada, for the next few nights. Beatty, a town known for its gambling history, would be my base for recording, since it is located just thirteen miles from Death Valley.

My field notes from that first morning in Death Valley on June 7, 2018, say this: *incredible silence, almost no jets, very few insects, no cars whatsoever and no people.* I was recording in Titus Canyon in the early morning hours. My recordings captured a (single?) fly, the faint rumble of my own stomach, an occasional piercing cry of a red-tailed hawk, the quiet hiss of the recording equipment and, well, endless nothing. Silence. After the wind in Ash Meadows the day before, and gusts at the mesquite dunes of Stovepipe Wells in Death Valley earlier in the morning, the silence was stunning. The air in the canyon was completely still. I had begun making field recordings in the hopes of capturing the silence evoked by monastic literature; here I thought I had found it, but it was somewhat tempered: a quiet place for sure, but silence as the pure absence of sound was still elusive. I could hear my own breathing, my own heartbeat. I found the stillness in Titus Canyon somewhat unsettling and in some of my recordings, I began to clap, just to hear in the still air reverberations against canyon walls.

My search for silence, like my quest for solitude, was both frustrated and disquieting. The paradox of solitude and community is deeply connected to that of silence and noise. Deserts, by their sheer extremes, amplify these contrasts. Sitting still and listening in the desert teaches us about the power of silence, and also the prevalence of noise. At the southern border of Death Valley lies the Fort Irwin National Training Center, and as I drove west out of the park and got out to take in the views of the valley, two military jets flew overhead, low and loud. I had reflected on these contrasts in the Negev Desert, too, where military jets and artillery practice reverberated even in remote oases. Study the maps of deserts around the world closely and you will frequently find military bases and toxic waste dumps. The "horizon of silence," as Sontag says, is elusive and fleeting even here.

## Perspectives on Noise and Silence

For as long as history has been recorded, humans have complained about noise. The scholar and poet Hillel Schwartz, in his book *Making Noise: From Babel to the Big Bang and Beyond*, writes about noise at the center of world religions' creation myths: "Out of primitive stillness, out of darkness, something disrupts the silence." The great sound of Om resounds at creation in Hindu myths. In the beginning, according to the biblical book of Genesis, a mighty wind spreads out over the still void and then God speaks, "Let there be light." An anonymous writer of an ancient book we now call Pseudo-Philo says, "Darkness and silence were before the world was made, and silence spoke a word and the darkness became light." The idea that a dark stillness, or more specifically a dark silence, existed at the beginning of time reflects, I think, a human longing for silence and also a deep sense of silence's power. From primordial silence, a first sound, a voice. These creation stories may also reveal why there is such a long and tangled history with noise.

At first glance, what is meant by "noise" may seem simple. Noise is, after all, mostly commonly defined as "unwanted sound." In this definition, noise may be jarring and harsh, steady irritating static, a clang in a quiet place, or the din of industry and transportation—whatever the precise sound, it is a sound that is unwanted. But this definition of noise depends on a person's perspective—one person's noise may be another's music. After all, some people use a "white noise" machine to lull them to sleep; others find the sound a grating annoyance.

The science writer Mike Goldsmith, in his 2012 book *Discord: The Story of Noise*, argues that part of the reason noise is so troubling is because of its association with danger: "For many millions of years," he writes, "loud, irregular sounds have signaled danger—the roar of volcanoes, the crackle of lightning, the rumble of earthquakes, the cries of hungry enemies. And instinctive reactions of fear and anger to loud sounds remain with us today, defining for us the concept of noise." Noise frequently engenders fear.

We have a heightened attention to noise these days, in part because we are learning more about how noise can negatively affect our health. The World Health Organization in Europe has argued that "excessive noise" is a serious threat to human health. Here in the United States, studies have shown that excessive exposure to noise not only causes hearing loss but also leads to heart disease, poor sleep, and hypertension. And noise seems to be everywhere. Around the world, a mysterious hum, a "droning sound" heard by 2 percent of the population, has been called "torture." Even the National Parks Service is doing extensive research on noise levels in remote wildernesses. Projects to mitigate the harmful effects of noise abound: pocket gardens, sound barriers along highways, and acoustic paneling in restaurants are just a few of the ways engineers and architects are addressing increasing noise. Museums, hospitals, and schools have attended to the impact of noise in their buildings. In our contemporary world it seems noise is more urgent and prevalent than ever. Although the phrase "noise pollution" has a decidedly modern ring to it, noise isn't a recent problem. The scale of the problem of noise may be worse than it was in the past, but the idea that noise can be detrimental is ancient.

But what about noise's apparent opposite—silence? Silence, like noise, is a potent ancient concept and also one with different perspectives. Although we may think of silence as an absence of all sound, the poet Ilya Kaminsky reminds us that "silence is an invention of the hearing." Silence, in my view, exists only in our imagination. Even the seemingly empty and desolate Titus Canyon in Death Valley was not silent, even anechoic chambers are not fully silent, even noise-cancelling headphones don't provide complete silence.

The artist Doug Wheeler's PSAD Synthetic Desert installation at the Guggenheim Museum in New York City in 2017 was a good illustration of this point. Wheeler had designed and installed a large room situated at the top of the museum as a quasi-anechoic chamber, intended to create an experience of silence in a vibrant and loud city. The walls were covered with sound-absorbing, soft, white, foam-like pyramidical cones, the floor space was carpeted, and visitors were only allowed in at timed intervals of ten or twenty minutes. Visitors were required to remove their shoes and to sit in one place for their allotted time with instructions to keep quiet. What was striking about the exhibit is that although the goal was silence, we each could hear our own bodies, our breathing and heartbeats, our stomachs, and the soft ventilation system of the museum itself. The experience was more about a quality of quiet stillness, hushing our own breath and settling our bodies, rather than silence.

For all our writings and reflections and poetry about silence, silence itself defies definition and we struggle to understand its meaning and our quest for it. In my own search for a definition of silence and a way to articulate an experience of silence, I have tried out a few ideas with my students: I suggest that silence might be an experience of expectancy and anticipation. Consider the moments between the flash of lightning and the crash of thunder. In those moments we wait, we expect the thunder, and we listen in a pregnant silence, even though the sounds of rain and wind may surround us. Silence here is our attention focused on an expected sound. I ask my students to think about silence and then I wait, not speaking, until one of them breaks the silence. Silence in a classroom, where it is expected that students and teacher will speak, can be intensely uncomfortable. And then I suggest another possibility: Might we think of silence not as absence but as the fullness of quiet, a blooming attention, moments where time slows? I'm drawn to the ideas of Native American writer N. Scott Momaday: "Silence . . . is the dimension in which ordinary and extraordinary events take their proper places." Our desire for silence, and even sometimes our discomfort with it, seems to me to be intimately tied to our sense of time and attention. Silence may offer us, in our hurried twenty-first century, a way to slow down and deeply sense where we are and who we are.

## Monastic Silence

Like us, ancient monks struggled with noise. Monks thought of noise in terms of disturbance—a sound that disturbed one's concentration: the din of demons or the clamor of pilgrims, eager to see the holy men "out in the desert." Some monastic texts complain about the distracting noise of children, the terror of roaring lions, the raucous sounds of visitors, the cacophony of monasteries themselves. Monastic rules regulated how much noise monks could make while eating and set strict limits on laughter.

Early Christian monks also complained about the noise of industry, the racket made by machines. For example, sometime in the seventh century, a strange story began to circulate about a wondrous and obedient camel in the Egyptian Desert. We are not quite sure about the storyteller, the date, or the exact location. But here is how the story went: visitors to a monastery in Egypt, arriving on horseback, were terrified when they encountered "huge dogs" growling along the monastery's walls. After being reassured that the dogs were under the authority of the *abba*—the leader of the monastery—the visitors entered the monastery. After praying with the monks, the visitors were taken to the monastery's well, where a camel, strapped to the water wheel, was standing still. They were surprised that the camel was not drawing water and asked why it had stopped. Here is what the monks told them: once the camel was drawing water during the time when the monks were called for prayers, and the noise of the water wheel drowned out the call, resulting in some monks missing the communal prayers in the church. So the camel was taught to stop drawing water whenever the monks were called to prayers.

It's possible that the kind of water wheel that is referred to in this story is one still in use in some parts of rural Egypt. Called a *saqiyyah* in Arabic, these water wheels can make loud creaking sounds, not unlike the metallic sounds of a windmill drawing water in desert ranches. The call to prayers for monks was given by pounding on the semantron. Still in use in monasteries around the world, the sound of a semantron reverberates well beyond the confines of monastery walls. What is striking to me about this story is how it reveals a concern about the noise of a machine covering the call to prayer, a noise that is so loud it silences the sound of the semantron. Sounds compete for monks' attention, and sometimes one needs to stop one noise so that another can be heard. The lessons of the seventh-century story aren't restricted to the ancient past: when new, especially loud train whistles were marketed to cross-country railroads in North America in the early twentieth century, one of the concerns was that their volume would obliterate the sounds of preachers. These stories aren't about noise and silence, but rather about which sounds command attention.

For ancient monks, prayer cultivated inner quiet attention and the practice of prayer was best supported by outer silence. The monastic literature speaks of silence in two primary ways. The first way of silence, we might say, was the idea of not speaking, of keeping silent. The *Sayings of the Desert*

*Fathers* emphasize time and again the importance of not speaking. Readers of the sayings are urged to control their tongues, keep "silence of the mouth," and not speak. Silence, in the sense of not speaking, is regarded as "the mother of wisest thoughts." Monastic texts tell of monks staying in their cells under a "discipline of silence" and dedicating themselves to prayer. In language that may seem decidedly modern, some sayings praise how a "lack of anxiety, keeping silent, and silent meditation bring forth purity." Ideas about the value and virtue of not speaking eventually made their way into later forms of monasticism, the most well known of which is the Cistercians (the Trappists) who practice a strict discipline of silence, of not speaking, in their monasteries.

Another story from the monastic literature speaks to the cultural context of this idea of "keeping silence." A monk tells a story of his parents. About his father he says: "Such was his silence that he seemed to have no voice to those who did not know him." On the other hand, he says, his mother "had so much conversation with everyone that her whole body seemed to be a tongue.'" His mother was a talker, we might say. When his father died, there was thunder, wind, and rain. And after his mother died, the monk wondered who he should be more like—his silent father or his talkative mother. He had a vision where he saw his father in "a great plain with many gardens, all sorts of fruits, and diverse trees of a beauty that defied description," and then he was shown "a dark and gloomy house filled with roaring and disturbance and a furnace ablaze" where he saw his mother and heard the sound of her voice. This vision answers his question about which parent he should emulate: surely his quiet father, who was rewarded with a beautiful afterlife. Such a story weighs silence and talkativeness, yes, but it is interwoven with cultural images of fathers and mothers, and gendered differences between male and female. What is striking is how silence and noise become reflected in images of bucolic heavenly gardens and the roar of hell's fire. A sensational story like this one served to provoke readers and to convince them to choose the way of silence.

There is another idea about silence in the monastic literature that moves beyond not speaking. Here a multivalent Greek word becomes essential to understanding monastic silence: *hesychia*, which could mean "silence," "solitude," "quiet," or "stillness." It was, and is, a simple word that took on deep significance for Christian monasticism in the eastern Mediterranean. *Hesychia* was contrasted with disturbance: practicing *hesychia* or living in *hesychia* meant freedom from disturbance—disturbance of noise, disturbance of distraction, the interruptions of sound. There are stories, for example, of monks who say, "The ones who pray to God should make their prayers in peace and *hesychia* and much tranquility." Essential to the idea of *hesychia* is a dualism: the inner and outer qualities of stillness and quiet. It required monks to reflect on how to develop inner quietude in the midst of a noisy and distracting world. This question was at the heart of the monastic endeavor.

One of the questions that emerges in the desert monastic literatures is whether *hesychia* is best practiced in a particular place. Is the desert, for example, more conducive to the practice of *hesychia* than the city? Here the tensions between the inner and outer experiences seem not fully resolved, for at times there are sayings that seem to suggest that an involvement in commerce, the practice of a profession, or an association with urban life prevents the practice of *hesychia*, while at other times there is the suggestion that the monk should be able to tend to and to cultivate *hesychia* in any kind of physical environment. The practice of cultivating *hesychia*—growing an inner sense of quiet, a stillness within—is a key contribution of the monastic life that is relevant today as we search for harmony between our inner lives and the outer world.

On several occasions, monastic sayings use agricultural images of growing plants and cultivating crops to describe the practice of *hesychia*. Consider the following: "An elder said, 'In the same way that no plant whatsoever grows upon a well-trodden highway, not even if you sow seed, because the surface is trodden down, so it is with us. Withdraw from all business into *hesychia* and you will see things growing that you did not know were in you, for you were walking on them.'" Here, the quality of inner stillness that is *hesychia* is something one tends and nurtures like a seedling. It can be walked upon and crushed, extinguished. Or it can be cared for so that it grows and blooms, blossoming in its freedom of movement. These metaphors illuminate the shifting landscapes of the inner life—how cultivating inner stillness is a practice continually in motion.

John Climacus, the seventh-century abbot of the Monastery of Saint Catherine in Sinai, the oldest continuously operating Christian monastery, is often credited with developing ideas of *hesychia* more fully than we see in the sayings of the Desert Fathers two centuries earlier. In fact, the scholar and Greek Orthodox bishop Kallistos Ware has highlighted just how integral *hesychia* is to John's treatise, called *The Ladder of Divine Ascent*: "*Hesychia* is a key word in John's doctrine of prayer, and the step which he devotes to it has proved, with the possible exception of Step 7 on the gift of tears, the most influential in the whole of *The Ladder*. By 'stillness' he means both an outward manner of life—that of the hermit or the solitary, living in a cell on his own—and also an inner disposition of continual prayer"; for John, Ware argues, "the journey is not outward and physical . . . but inward and spiritual into the sanctuary of the heart."

To read *The Ladder of Divine Ascent* is to be confronted with the sense that monasticism is a living practice of cultivating the inner life even in the midst of distractions, noise, and busyness. John Climacus writes that "the beginning of *hesychia* is the shaking off of all crashes [noisiness] as something that will shake [disturb] the depths of the soul. The end is when one is not afraid of the disturbances." *Hesychia*, for John, is simultaneously near the top rung of the ladder of divine ascent and the deepest realms of monastic practice: "He who has achieved *hesychia*," he writes, "has arrived at the very center of the mysteries, but he would never have reached these depths if he had not first seen and heard the sound of the waves and of the evil spirits, if he had not even been splashed by those waters. . . . The ear of the hesychast will hear wonders from God." John's eloquent connections between solitude, listening, and wonder are unmistakable in these passages.

The hesychasm that was born in Christian monasticism in the Middle East long ago spread to central Asia, throughout the Eastern Orthodox church, Western Europe, and well beyond. In the modern area, the Trappist monk, theologian, and prolific writer Thomas Merton is probably the best example of the impact of hesychasm throughout Christian monasticism—in the East and in the West. Merton drew parallels between the Buddhist practices of Zen and the ideas of the Christian Desert Fathers in writing about contemplative practice. And, for Merton, the essential meaning of *hesychia*—beyond the ideals of solitude, stillness—was its "deeply simple way of prayer."

In his 1962 lectures on hesychasm delivered to his fellow monks at the Abbey of Gethsemani in Kentucky, Merton said this:

The effect of sun on the stones and light and shadow, these are things that you don't pay too much attention to, but they're healthy and they create a certain atmosphere of silence. They help interior silence. You can't have interior silence just by pressing a button and saying "got to have interior silence." You have got to live in an atmosphere propitious for interior silence. The irreplaceable thing for that is just simply nature.

This is a powerful claim about how essential nature is, "the stones and light and shadow," for cultivating inner silence. During the lectures, Merton sometimes paused to listen for a sound coming from outside—for example, at one point the song of a Carolina wren. His writings compel us to ask, again: What *is* the relationship between place and the cultivation of inner quietude, *hesychia*? And can the natural world with its "atmosphere of silence" offer solace in a world of noise?

## Silence in Nature and the Contemplative Life

The field recordist Gordon Hempton, known as the "Sound Tracker," has long been an activist for preserving quiet natural places. At times the definitions he uses for noise and silence can seem simplistic: noise, for Hempton, is human sound, including planes, trains, trucks, and even human voices in what he calls "pristine nature"; silence is the quiet and "pure" sound of nature without any human interruption.

In 2005 Hempton founded the project "One Square Inch of Silence" in the Hoh Rain Forest of the Olympic Mountain range in Washington State. Located a three-mile hike from the Visitors' Center in a forest glade, Hempton sought to create a natural place free from all human noise. The website for the project now suggests that the place "is very possibly the quietest place in the United States." In his book *One Square Inch of Silence* where he discusses the project, Hempton had this to say about his goal: "By keeping even one square inch 100 percent free of noise, or at least attempting to do so, I am able to push back aircraft for many miles and help to preserve natural quiet over much of the entire park. Natural quiet, like clean air and clean water, is part of a delicate ecosystem." A delicate acoustical ecosystem. But, of course, Hempton's definition of silence is not a pure absence of all sounds. He quests for birdsong and wind, oceans and river sounds, and the subtle cadences of natural soundscapes. He is after an "atmosphere of silence," to return to Merton's phrase.

In 2012, when I was in the early stages of fieldwork and research for this book, I visited the Benedictine Monastery of Christ in the Desert located in northwestern New Mexico on the very fringes of the Colorado Plateau. Thomas Merton visited the monastery in 1968, just four years after its founding. Located down a thirteen-mile-long dirt road and surrounded by miles of protected wilderness, calling the monastery remote is an understatement. The town of Abiquiu, made famous by the artist Georgia O'Keeffe who lived nearby at Ghost Ranch and who was a frequent visitor to the monastery, is located nearly thirty miles away. At many times of the year, during winter snows and summer monsoons, the road is not drivable. Merton described the monastery like this: "In America, there is no monastic foundation which has found so perfect a desert setting as that of the Chama Canyon, in New Mexico. . . . The place was chosen with careful deliberation, and it is admirable." A pamphlet about the monastery emphasizes the "solitude and quiet" of the place. The prior of the monastery at its founding, Father Aelred Wall, had this to say about the relationship between a place like the remote desert and monastic practice: "A monastery is not a refuge, not a solution to problems of adjustment. Monasticism is a head-on collision with reality, and the more silent, the more solitude, the more head-on it is."

Christ in the Desert seemed like a perfect place for me to record and to listen as I sought to understand how natural sounds impacted ancient monasticism. After visiting the cool interior of the striking adobe church, designed by the Japanese architect George Nakashima, and listening to the quiet interior—no voices, few footsteps—I stepped back out into the bright sun to walk the stations of the cross. Here I made my first set of recordings, trying to capture an acoustic imprint of the monastery grounds. On that day, midmorning, I heard the croak of ravens echoing off the five-hundred-foot steep walls of Mesa de las Viejas behind the monastery and the flapping of their wings overhead when they flew low, a rooster crowing beyond the gardens, the buzz of flies, and some soft voices coming from other visitors to the monastery. A prop plane also flew overhead—even in this remote canyon, the sound of planes is now part of the "silence."

If there is a signature sound for the place, a sound distinctive and unique to the monastery grounds, it seemed to me to be the Chama River. The sound of water in the desert is always striking, unexpected, even surprising in drylands. The mud-colored waters flowed quickly, and I sat on the red sandy banks listening to the river and to the birds singing and fluttering in the shrubs. And, again, a small plane overhead. Noise amid the silence? A broken quiet? It depends, in part, on one's perspective. The siting of desert monasteries requires water resources: a creek, a spring, deep wells—water is a necessity for humans, animals, and plants in this harsh landscape. The sound of water at many desert monasteries is a key sound—whether in fountains as I noted at Saint Anthony's

Monastery in the Sonoran Desert or here at Christ in the Desert in New Mexico. The grounds of the monastery seemed lush for the high desert, but this, too, is a feature of monasticism from its beginnings: monks cultivated gardens, making the desert bloom, an idea that is at least as old as parts of the Bible, where in the Book of Isaiah it says: "The wilderness and the dry land shall be glad, the desert shall rejoice and blossom."

Over time, I began to rethink my own ideas about silence as absence. As I listen to the rich sonority of desert landscape, I quest less for silence and more for a quality of presence, and perhaps even "excess." Sara Maitland suggests a similar sentiment in her *A Book of Silence*:

> Whether we see silence as the way to access these states—that is, whether we see it as a liminal state or a doorway—or whether we see silence as the autonomous space within which these experiences are happening, we cannot just say this is void or negative; that all silence is waiting—or wanting, needing, yearning—to be broken. Or that it ought to be broken.

> Silence does not seem to be a loss or lack of language. I have found it to be a whole world in and of itself, alongside of, woven within language and culture, but independent of it. It comes from a different place altogether.

A silence born of presence and attention, atmospheres of silence, silences that manifest a whole world—these images of silence seem all the more urgent in our busy modern lives. Perhaps we can best think of silence as a kind of pause, like the musical rest, which does not so much speak to absence but has a rhythmic voice all its own.

## CODA

Silence as the absence of all sound rarely exists. A windless canyon might seem silent until a single hawk punctuates the air. The quiet sounds of a raven echoing off cliff walls, insects, a lone rooster; or the crickets and doves in a remote cemetery—these too are desert silences. Other times, it's the quiet of expectation after the lightning and before a peal of thunder. Sit quietly for long enough and what seems like silence becomes a subtle presence: birds, flies, wind, the waning storm.

# 4

# MONASTIC DESERT
# SOUNDSCAPES

*Now I will do nothing but listen . . .*
*I hear all sounds running together, combined, fused or*
*following . . .*
—Walt Whitman, *Song of Myself*

After my early-morning recording session in solitude at Santa
Elena Canyon along Big Bend's Rio Grande River was interrupted by an arriving tour bus, I moved on to locations eastward along the river and then north and east along the Ross
Maxwell Scenic Drive. I was frustrated by the confluence
of sounds, dissonant with the quiet I had found earlier: the
sounds of the bus arriving and keeping its motor running,
yes, and the nasal whizz of chainsaws working to clear brush
downriver; the sounds of cattle grazing and the clang of their
bells; motorcyclists roaring through the park; the near-con-
stant din of patrol planes. I had thought here in these desert
borderlands I would capture the natural sounds of the Chihuahuan Desert, the last of the four North American deserts
that I had yet to record. I stopped in at the Castolon Visitor
Center where I found a book of nature writing about Big
Bend with the title: *God's Country or Devil's Playground.* The
title alone spoke to me perfectly of the paradox I found in
monastic literatures about the desert, so I purchased it and
moved on. Later I read the excerpt in the book taken from

geologist Robert T. Hill's record of his 1901 survey of the Rio Grande, how the river flowed in side canyons "noiselessly," "with hardly a ripple or gurgle," while at other locations it made a "roaring noise," "a tremendous roaring sound like distant thunder." The sound of a train's whistle initially gave him comfort in the midst of the cacophonous river—until he realized it was a distress call from the train.

I pulled in at Burro Mesa Pouroff and saw only one other car, a hopeful sign that I might be relatively alone. Maybe here I'd be able to make some recordings of the natural surroundings. I hiked in toward Javelina Wash carrying my recording equipment and camera and sat for a long time recording the sounds of a mockingbird singing through his morning repertoire, varied and relentless. My attention was on that bird, even as the wind picked up and as the air warmed and insects and other birds began to add to the sonorous landscape. This was the kind of soundscape I hoped to capture—natural, vibrant, and without human sounds. I found a soundscape where sounds were, in Whitman's words, "running together, combined, fused."

Later in the morning I tried another location—the Sam Nail Ranch. Although the ranch hasn't been occupied since World War II, a windmill still draws water, attracting a variety of birds. In the midday wind, the creaking and rhythmic sound of the windmill, the trickle of water, and the gusts of wind through pecan and cottonwood trees dominated the soundscape. A few birds darted about, but it was the windmill and wind that were most prominent, and I was reminded of the story from John Moschos about the camel who was trained to stop drawing water at the time for prayers so that the sound of the machine didn't drown out the call to prayer and the psalm singing. Slowly, I began to rethink my methods of recording, how my goals had been somewhat artificial—namely, to capture a "pure and pristine" natural soundscape without any human sounds, including sounds of machines like wind-mills and chainsaws, buses and planes and motorcycles.

I read an interview with the daughter of Sam Nail who talked about how her family's ranch was bought by the National Park Service around the year 1943, how they tore down the ranch, leaving only one adobe wall that now stands. She thought that the NPS destroyed the ranch in an attempt to "obliterate every sign of human habitation." I kept return-ing to my own frustrations, how I too was hoping to "oblit-erate" humans from my recordings. I began to wonder if I wasn't missing an essential lesson from both my practice of field recording and from my reading of desert monastic liter-atures: humans have always been a part of desert environ-ments, and part of the history of deserts is also the history of humans. One of the ways to learn about these essential in-terrelationships of humans and deserts is through the com-ingling of sounds in a rich and sonorous landscape.

## Two Ways to Listen to Nature

When we listen to the natural world, *how* we listen influences what we hear. Is our attention drawn to the ambient surround sound (Whitman's "sounds running together") or do we focus on one particular sound? Can we take it all in or does our attention zero in, perhaps on something we find distracting or unusual or pleasant? These two ways of listening to natu-ral sounds—the ambient and the singular—have been cru-cial to artistic and scientific discoveries, and they provide an important insight into how monks were shaped by listening to the natural world.

Acoustic ecology and bioacoustics, two fields of study that rely on the techniques of field recordings, can deepen our sense of possibilities for listening. Although these two fields today regard each other as distinct in very important ways, and sometimes with a measure of suspicion, both fields inform my own understanding of ancient desert monastic sounding worlds. They teach us about ways to listen to ambient soundscapes and how to uncover deep understanding of particular sounds, such as the sound of a single bird or bird species, or the sound of an insect, mammal, or amphibian.

In 1973, the composer R. Murray Schafer founded the World Soundscape Project at Simon Fraser University in Vancouver, British Columbia. Schafer's work marked the beginnings of a field of study that eventually came to be called Acoustic Ecology; even more broadly, he is sometimes regarded as the founder of sound studies. Along with a team of young researchers, Schafer wanted to document the changing soundscapes of Vancouver as well as to understand the relationship between the sounding world and the world of composition. He was especially concerned about the increasing noise in the city, especially aircraft and automobile traffic. As a composer, Schafer was also influenced by the experimental work of composers like John Cage, who famously said, "Music is sounds, sounds around us whether we're in or out of the concert halls." Schafer wrote with enthusiasm about these early influences in his 1977 book called *The Soundscape: Our Sonic Environment and the Tuning of the World*: "Today all sounds belong to a continuous field of possibilities," he wrote, "lying *within the comprehensive dominion of music*. Behold the new orchestra: the sonic universe!"

The idea that the soundscapes around us could be seen as music and that musical compositions could draw experimentally on recorded soundscapes—including city life, environmental sounds, the sounds of an audience within a music hall—have continued to influence this field of study. Acoustic ecology, also known as soundscape ecology, was defined by the World Soundscape Project's *Handbook for Acoustic*

*Ecology*, edited by Barry Truax, one of Schafer's researchers and later his successor at Simon Fraser, as "the study of the effects of the acoustic environment, or soundscape, on the physical responses or behavioral characteristics of those living within it." Put simply, acoustic ecologists—and now the field is wide, diverse, and international—study how sound shapes human behavior and experience.

More recently, in a *BioScience* article published in 2011, entitled "Soundscape Ecology: The Science of Sound in the Landscape," soundscape ecology is defined as "all sounds, those of biophony, geophony, and anthrophony, emanating from a given landscape to create unique acoustical patterns across a variety of spatial and temporal scales." The term *geophony* here refers to the sounds of the earth, such as wind, water, thunder; *biophony* means the sounds made by animals, including mammals, birds, reptiles, amphibians; and *anthrophony* (also sometimes called *anthropophony*) is the varied and diverse sounds made by humans, including the human voice. Although not all acoustic ecologists are composers or specifically work in the area of soundscape research and music, a strong tie to music and the arts remains part of the field.

By contrast, *bioacoustics*, also sometimes called *animal acoustics*, is a scientific field within the biological sciences that studies animal communication. Scientists in this field have long studied individual animal species, including their modes of sound production and communication, the ways in which their changing environment impacts the sounds they produce, different kinds of vocalizations within a particular species (for example, birdsong and bird alarm calls), and the "signature sounds" of individuals within a species. According to its website, *Bioacoustics* is a scientific journal specifically devoted to "the scientific study, recording and analysis of animals sounds." Like acoustic ecology, bioacoustics has increasingly examined how climate change, habitat destruction, and increasing noise affects animal acoustics and animal communication.

As I mentioned previously, my own entry into the techniques and practice of field recording was through the Bioacoustics Research Program at Cornell University's Lab of Ornithology. The Lab, which also houses the largest digital archive of natural sounds in the world, The Macaulay Library of Natural Sounds, annually offers workshops in natural sound recording techniques and analysis. I first participated in their natural sound recording workshop in 2013 when it was led by Greg Budney, the curator of the Macaulay Library, and Bill McQuay, a former NPR Radio Expeditions writer, field recordist, and audio engineer. It was held at San Francisco State University's beautiful field campus along the North Yuba River in the Sierra Nevada mountains of California. The course was designed to train scientists in the techniques of field recording, with the biologists studying the alarm calls of chipmunks, the songs of katydids and crickets, the dawn chorus of birds. But it also attracted folks like me, who loved listening to natural sounds and hoped to use recordings for art, history, or poetry. With our early-morning recording sessions in the forests and meadows of the Sierra Nevada mountains, this workshop was a feast for my ears and taught me so much about how to listen and how to capture what I was hearing with the use of a digital recorder and set of microphones.

I returned for a few days of the workshop again in the summer of 2018, in part because I hoped to meet one of the most important scientists of birdsong—Donald Kroodsma, formerly a professor of biology at the University of Massachusetts. In his 2005 *The Singing Life of Birds*, Kroodsma offers readers insights into individual birds and their songs and, along the way, teaches readers about listening: "Each story," he writes about his selection of particular birds, "is based on listening and on learning how to hear an individual bird use its sounds, and each story illustrates some of the fundamentals of the science called 'avian bioacoustics.'" The book, along with its accompanying CD, renders our most common backyard birds (think robins), exquisitely and profoundly interesting.

Having read Don Stap's book, *Birdsong: A Natural History*, where he details Kroodsma's meticulous and tireless work to capture birdsong, I found myself intimidated to meet Kroodsma and his partner Janet at the workshop in the Sierra Nevada mountains. But they were warm and encouraging about my historical project and my love of field recording. I had to leave the workshop early, and we communicated by email a few days later. It turns out they left early, too, because, according to Kroodsma, "the birds just weren't singing quite enough for me, to get the kind of information and stories that I like to squeeze out of them."

I have thought a lot about this exchange with Kroodsma and my desire to understand what listening to natural sounds today can teach us about the past. I have also wondered, as I read the monastic literatures of antiquity, whether ancient monks might also teach us a kind of acoustic ecological *and* bioacoustical listening. Monks did not have recording technologies, of course, but they did tune their ears to the sounds of their environment. Their stories reveal an ancient attention to the full ambience of place as well as keen attention to particular sounds.

## Listening to Ancient Monks' Soundscapes

What did ancient monks hear in their environment? And what did they learn from these sounds? How did these sounds shape their sense of where and who they were within desert landscapes? Can we hear an ancient soundscape by reading sayings and stories from monastic literatures? And what might we learn about the ancient environmental world through this kind of practice? In the pages that follow, I will attend closely to the ways in which our monastic texts reveal both ancient soundscapes and the deep connection monks had with their environment.

Behind many of the sayings and stories of the Desert Fathers about the sounds of the desert lies a repertoire of biblical passages that speak to howling and destructive winds, God's voice that thunders or that sounds like waters, the melodious song of birds, or sheer silence in the heavens. One of the most important biblical books for monks was the Book of Psalms, which speaks poetically and expressively about seas roaring, trees of the forest singing, mountains breaking forth with joy, and fields exulting—all in praise to the divine. These psalms were in the minds of monks in late antiquity who memorized and meditated on them, copied and recited them.

Some monks would also have read poetic books like *The Wisdom of Solomon*, a book that was probably written several hundred years before Christian monasticism began. It came to be preserved and read by Christians, and many of its motifs find their way into the desert monastic literatures. *The Wisdom of Solomon* provides a vivid example of ancient acoustic ecology in a passage that is partly a retelling of the biblical story of the Israelite's rescue from slavery in Egypt and partly a discussion of the differences between the Egyptians and the Israelites. Listen to how the writer describes the Egyptians who were bound in "one chain of darkness" in the desert:

Whether there came a whistling wind,
or a melodious sound of birds in wide-spreading
    branches,
or the rhythm of violently rushing water,
or the harsh crash of rocks hurled down,

or the unseen running of leaping animals,
or the sound of the most savage roaring beasts,
or an echo thrown back from a hollow of the mountains,
it paralyzed them with terror. For the whole world
was illumined with brilliant light, and went about its
   work unhindered,
while over those people alone heavy night was spread.

The Egyptians, the enemies of the "holy ones" according to this book, experienced a loud and terrifying array of desert sounds, and hearing these sounds, but being unable to see, is inextricably tied to their identity as the enemy of the Israelites. The landscape of the desert here is sensory and sensational and powerful. What interests me most is the ranging repertoire of sounds: the whistling wind, melodious birds, rhythms of water, crash of rocks, footsteps and roaring of animals, echoes against the mountains. Together, these sounds paint an ambient, acoustic ecology of the desert. They also tie hearing to identity: the Egyptians hear these sounds, but they do not see the rocks or animals. They know who they are because they can hear these terrifying sounds. In the ancient world, hearing, like seeing, was tied to understanding and knowing. We say, "I hear you," when we want to convey to someone that we understand what they are saying and that we identify; the ancients did the same.

The sounds that are described in this passage are ones that we find in the monastic texts, too. We can begin with wind, which Lyall Watson notes, in his 1985 book called *Heaven's Breath*, is an important acoustical motif with a long history: in the ancient world as in today's world, wind can be hot and scorching, beating and violent, bucolic and gentle, seductive and dangerous, bitterly cold and deathly; winds can whistle and hiss, howl, screech, crash, caress, shake, rattle, and roll; winds blow from the south, north, east and west—each direction offering its own resonances and attributes; winds are favorable and adverse; winds are always unpredictable. Wind is, put simply, "moving air," as Watson says. It is also air with mercurial changeability.

In antiquity, wind was potent with significance and meaning. Winds could signal divine affection or divine condemnation. Monks spoke of tornado-like winds, powerful enough to send rocks crashing. At other times, they spoke of a gentler wind, heard through vegetation. Consider the following passage from the *Sayings of the Desert Fathers*:

> One day Abba Arsenius came to a place where there were reeds moving in the wind. The old man said to the brothers, "What is this shaking?" They said, "Some reeds." Then the old man said to them, "When one who is sitting in *hesychia* hears the voice of the sparrow, his heart no longer experiences the same *hesychia*. How much worse it is when you hear the movement of those reeds."

On its simplest level, this saying reveals something about the desert soundscape: reeds, probably along the Nile river, moving in the wind and quaking with sounds; and then there is the particular sound of a bird, a sparrow. The passage speaks to the challenges of cultivating inner stillness in the midst of the surrounding noisy soundscape. I have thought of this passage frequently while recording the sounds of winds in reeds at Ash Meadows in Nevada, at ponds in Guadalupe National Park in Texas, and at springs in the Negev Desert. The sounds of wind in the reeds is surely one of the signature sounds of desert life, especially at watering holes.

The fourth-century writer Paphnutius in his *Histories of the Monks of Upper Egypt* tells the story of a monk named Isaac who lived on an island in the middle of the Nile River. When travelers went to see Isaac, Paphnutius says, they needed to pass "the huge rocks lying in the water in the middle of the river, where the waters roared in a terrifying manner." The terrifyingly loud waters test the travelers' resolve, and they hint at one of the desert's sound bites. There are still places along the Nile River today where rapids create deafening sounds. If deserts are defined in part by their lack of water, they are also paradoxically defined by the times in which water is torrential, destructive, and terrifyingly loud. The sound of water in the desert is one of extremes: a deathly silence during drought or the roar of floods during the winter or monsoon seasons.

Thunder, too, is a dramatic sound in the desert, especially if that desert landscape has little foliage or soft sand dunes to muffle its reverberation. The idea of thunder as a sign is one of the most ancient ideas about natural sounds: thunder was a sign from heaven; it was voice of the divine, sometimes displeased. Monastic texts speak similarly of thunder accompanying a person's death, especially a monk's death, or the sound accompanying a vision in the darkest night. Thunder was closely associated with the sound of the earth quaking— *seismos* is the Greek word, from which we get our word *seismographs*, instruments that measure earthquakes. The sound associated with shaking, a reverberant vibration, seems to have been one of the keynotes for ancient monks. Even the reeds, as we have already seen, quake in the wind.

What about the sounds of animals in the desert—the desert biophonies? There are an array of stories about monks who hear and learn from the sounds of roaring lions, the howl of wolves, bellowing camels, and the bark of hyenas. Take, for example, the story of the monk Macarius who hears the cries of a wolf and regards them as the cries of suffering humanity. Or the story that comes to be told in many different versions about a monk who was walking one day and came upon a lion, roaring in pain. The monk discovered that the lion had a thorn in its paw, he sat down to take out the thorn, and afterward the lion followed the monk as a faithful disciple. This story might seem like fanciful fiction, but it helps us understand how human imagination yearns for the possible, reaches for surprise, for a symbiotic relationship between human and animal, monk and lion, in an extreme desert landscape.

The sound of birds—sparrows, eagles, crows, ravens— appear in many texts. In a story about the fifth-century leader of the White Monastery in Egypt, Apa Shenoute, we read about a raven that came down to sit on the wall above Shenoute while he was seated talking with some visitors. The raven croaks at the men. And then the monks begin to discuss whether it is important to listen to the raven or not, whether the raven holds a message from God or whether the raven is just looking for a meal. Apa Shenoute instructs them: "Do not again put it in your heart to listen to this bird. He is only calling to the Lord to get his dinner ready!" Ravens are ubiquitous in deserts and they do frequently congregate in places where humans settle. The story at Egypt's White Monastery blends well with what we know about raven behavior.

The biologist Bernd Heinrich writes in his 1999 book *Mind of the Raven* about the way of "ravens that permits or encourages an uncanny closeness to develop with humans." What Heinrich speaks about here is not new: humans have a long history of relationships with ravens, extending well back into biblical times. In fact, there are striking resonances with biblical stories in the monastic texts about ravens. Of course, Noah's sending out a raven after the flood would have been in the minds of monks, but also the ravens that fed the prophet Elijah in the first Book of Kings and the cries of young ravens found in the Book of Psalms.

The geophonies and biophonies of monastic soundscapes are illuminating. But what about the anthropophonies? The sounds of humans are one of the most prominent features of monastic texts, often in the context of complaints about noise. The human voice is evocative, varied, and essential for monasticism: the multilingual voices of visitors, the voices of other monks, the voices of children. But there are also the voices of monks themselves and their chanting of prayers, psalms, hymns, and liturgies. It is true that monastic texts encourage monks not to speak, and yet their voices were audible everywhere. Reverberant chapels were carved in caves or built on the sides of cliffs, which amplified monks' voices. Many of the complaints about noise, as we saw in the last chapter, were about the sounds of monks themselves—their footsteps walking along paths to and from the monastery, the sounds they made as they worked in the monastery gardens.

Over time, as monks established themselves within the desert landscape, they began to see themselves as part of the desert—a desert with a long human history by the time they arrived. They sometimes settled in ruins that were still fresh with echoes of those who had come before; sometimes they built new structures, created new soundscapes with the technologies essential to their shared lives; and, frequently, they lived their monastic lives in close proximity to and surrounded by non-monastic residents of these deserts.

## Seeing Ourselves as Part of Nature

In 1964, President Lyndon B. Johnson signed into law the Wilderness Act "in order to assure that an increasing population, accompanied by expanding settlement and growing mechanization, does not occupy and modify all areas within the United States and its possessions, leaving no lands designated for preservation and protection in their natural conditions." The language of this Act is both inspired and problematic in its definition of "wilderness," as "an area where the earth and its community of life are untrammeled by man, where man himself is a visitor who does not remain." Much has been written about this piece of legislation and especially the way it has constructed "wilderness" as pristine and untouched, a "sense of nature as a picturesque commodity," as Alison Byerly has suggested. So, too, Gary Snyder, in *The Practice of the Wild*, reminds us that: "It has always been part of basic human experience to live in a culture of wilderness. There has been no wilderness without some kind of human presence for several hundred thousand years. Nature is not a place to visit, it is *home*." We need to rethink the human-wilderness divide in fundamental ways. The use of terms like "wilderness" or "wild" or "nature" has depended upon the erasure of peoples and histories—whole stretches of the dwelt-in desert are obscured by these erasures and the stark distinction between humans and nature. The truth is that humans have lived in remote deserts for as long as humans have existed, and we continually erase the presence of those who have come before us.

My frustration at not being able to capture the sounds of "pristine wilderness" in field recordings is bound up with the artificial idea that nature is out there separate from humans. And that the desert is empty. I longed for, and still do long for, the quiet of nature; planes and automobiles thwarted my attempts at a "pure" environmental recording. The ancient monks revealed their embeddedness within a sonorous desert, even as they also expressed resentment of the distracting sounds of humans. Their stories are filled with longing, but they also offer a rich sense of lives lived in ambient locations. The sounds of the desert need to be understood as "running together, combined," to return to Whitman's poem; the desert soundscapes the monks heard was a comingling of the geophonies, biophonies, *and* anthropophonies.

The idea of wilderness as that place "untrammeled by man" only holds if we erase the history of those who have come before us. Petroglyphs and rock paintings in deserts around the world speak to a rich history of human-desert cohabitation. And so I return to my recordings, which teach me that humans are part of this landscape. The windmill at the Sam Nail ranch in Big Bend National Park is as much a part of the desert soundscape now as the sound of the camel drawing water at the monastery long ago in Egypt. I learn to listen for the ways that humans appear in my recordings with less frustration and more curiosity.

Acoustic ecology and bioacoustics have so much to teach us about listening. So, too, do the monks who heard the desert soundscape and listened. If we regard ourselves as part of nature, as part of the desert, as partly responsible for its long history and its future, might we then also see our impact more clearly and come to rethink our separateness from the natural world? Deep listening is one route to a more nuanced and subtle understanding of inextricable ties that bind us to our world.

## CODA

The vibrant ambience of desert soundscapes is dynamic and ever changing. From the winds blowing through reeds at a desert spring to the raspy calls of grasshoppers on arid hillsides—all is constantly shifting. Listen closely to the interplay of birds, thunder, and the arrival of rain. Ephemeral streams flow seasonally and replenish parched landscapes. And almost always there are the sounds of humans, perhaps most vivid in the rumble and blare of a passing train.

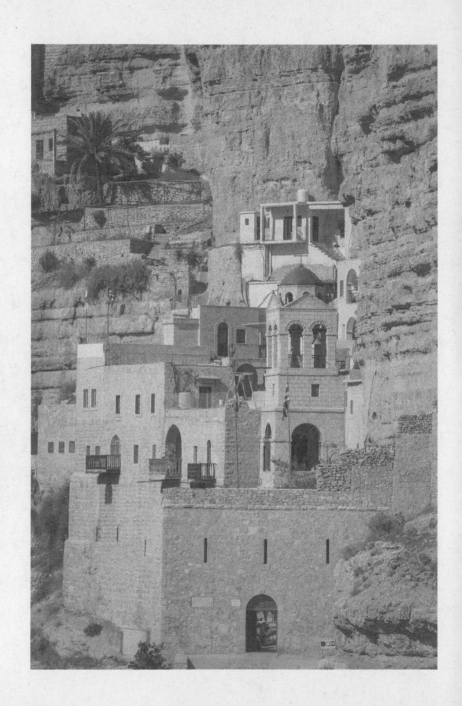

# 5
# ECHOES IN
# SACRED CANYONS

the remembered canyon silence. It is a stillness
like no other I have experienced,
for at the very instant of bouncing
and echoing every slight noise
off cliffs and around bends,
the canyons swallow them.
—Wallace Stegner, *The Sound of Mountain Water*

Yea though I walk through the valley
of the shadow of death,
I will fear no evil
—Psalm 23:4

In the spring of 2014, on a field recording trip to the Negev
and Judean deserts of southern Israel, I spent a day at the
Greek Orthodox monastery called Saint George of Choziba,
located in Wadi Qilt in the Judean Desert just east of
Jerusalem. As far as we can tell, the monastic history of this
wadi, or canyon, began in the early fifth century when a
group of hermits settled there in caves in the limestone
canyon walls, which run roughly parallel to and just to the
north of the modern road from Jerusalem to Jericho. But
the canyon has a long and storied history stretching back at
least to biblical times; trails along its rim and floor have

been used for thousands of years. Today, the monastery is a spectacular example of a cliff monastery, hanging roughly midway between the floor of the canyon and its rim. As the canyon runs westward toward the Jordan River, near where it meets the Dead Sea, the remains of hermit "cells" (caves) are visible and are still sometimes used by monks in the monastery. They were connected to one another by a narrow path from the monastery. Some of these cave-cells were fairly elaborate, built with mosaic floors and front-facing courtyards containing cisterns for water and mud ovens for cooking. Other hermitages along the cliffs were quite simple.

I arrived in the early morning, while the air was still cool, with a friend and colleague of mine, a scholar of Byzantine monasticism named Chrysi Kotsifou, who was on a fellow-ship in Jerusalem at the time. A friend of hers also joined us for the day. We pulled into the parking lot along the southern rim of the canyon, unloaded my recording gear, and were met by locals hoping we would hire their mules to get down to the monastery. The hike, we said, was fairly short and we would be fine. I was already beginning to worry that my goal of recording birdsong and canyon river waters would be impeded by the presence of so many people in the area—especially given the fact that the canyon's steep walls create a kind of echo chamber that carries the sounds of voices and footsteps far distances. Reverberance is a mixed blessing here.

We made our way down the trail, finally coming to the bridge that crosses the creek. Just above the bridge we could look across the canyon and see the monastery itself with its bell tower's burgundy, domed roof. The morning was alive with sonority, and I was eager to record the sounds of the breeze through palm trees, the starlings and doves and ravens, and the brilliant echoes of the canyon. But I was also worrying. As the morning wore on, more and more visitors arrived and the sounds of voices and footsteps were becoming louder. Sure enough, as soon as I set up my recording equipment, put my headphones on, and pressed record I could hear human chatter and the clatter of rocks scattering as pilgrims were arriving by mule and foot to the monastery.

We pressed on toward the north side of the canyon and hiked up to the monastery, seemingly hanging from the cliff. Above the monastery we saw what's known as the hermitage of a monk named Gabriel—its thatched walls and the ladder leading to it still visible. Looking to the south, into the canyon that eventually leads to the Jordan River Valley and the city of Jericho, all seemed desolate and barren. By contrast, the canyon's floor and the gardens tended by the monks were lush, cool, and inviting.

Visitors to the monastery are greeted in an open reception area just outside the main church, a chapel dedicated to the Virgin Mary. When we arrived, others were already there admiring the views, and enjoying the cool shade of the monastery. The limestone walls were like an amphitheater amplifying all the sounds—voices, birds, water, and wind.

I didn't expect to spend the morning talking with the abbot of the monastery, Father Konstantinos. But Kotsifou, Greek Orthodox herself, knew the monks at the monastery and conversed easily with Father Konstantinos in their shared native tongue of modern Greek. She told him of my interest in recording the sounds of Wadi Qilt and my curiosity about desert sounds and the lives of monks. His first response was to take out his cell phone and say that he had been trying to record the sounds of the wadi, too. He spoke about the sounds of frogs, of grouse in the late afternoon, and the terrifying, loud rushing river during the previous winter's torrential downpours. He also told a story about a helicopter that landed in the wadi to rescue a hiker some years back. Father Konstantinos spoke, too, about a particular starling that had for years come to tap on his window and how he had tapped back, recorded the bird's whistling tunes, and how, one day, the starling didn't return. He also remarked, strikingly in contrast to the stories of Antony in Egypt, that "only demons and snakes are silent." The desert, for him, seemed to be alive with sound.

I'm not exactly sure when I began to rethink my singular focus on capturing "natural sounds" in the desert, but I do look back on this day as a pivotal moment. The monks offered to knock the wooden board used to call monks for prayers, the semantron, so that I could record its rhythms and hear its echoes down the canyon. They also sang the Anastasia, a hymn to Mary, in their acoustically rich chapel. Here I recorded what is surely one of the most important of desert monastic sounds—the sounds of the liturgy. The monks do not permit pictures of themselves, but they were warmly hospitable and glad to sing for my recorder.

I listen to these recordings now with ears tuned to the sense of place. Because it wasn't a regular church service, at the beginning of the recording of an Akathist, one can hear the visitors outside the chapel continuing to talk with one another. Their voices carry easily into the resonant chapel. But once the monks begin to sing a few lines and the rich sound of their voices carries beyond the chapel, all falls silent outside. The visitors cease talking and the monks' chant resounds throughout the monastery and beyond. I began the morning with a clear sense of what I wanted to capture in my recordings—birds, wind, water—and I left the monastery with recordings that would in the following months make me rethink my own intentions. I was beginning to formulate a fuller sense of the acoustic ecology in the monastic desert, one that requires us to include the sounds of humans.

Wadi Qilt and the monastery of Saint George of Choziba, one of our best-documented monasteries in the Judean Desert, have much to teach us about how humans have occupied desert canyons. Canyons, wadis, narrow valleys—these are especially rich geological places that invite reflection, again, on paradox and the profound ways that place shaped monastic practice. Some canyons are claustrophobically narrow and dangerous in times of flash flooding. Others are rich with plant and animal life in river bottoms. Canyons inspire and terrify, speak to grandeur and desolation, reverberate with sound and with history, and they are sometimes utterly silent.

"Ithaca is Gorges" is the saying associated with the town where I live most of the year in New York's Finger Lakes; my walk to campus crosses the two-hundred-foot-deep Fall Creek Gorge. There is no question that canyons can be beautiful. But they are also treacherous. I think of this every time I cross the swaying suspension bridge. From rim to canyon floor, canyons offer multiple perspectives on life, nature, and our sounding worlds. What do monastic literatures have to say about canyons and Wadi Qilt in particular? How might these evocative landscapes give us insights into our own longings and fears? And how might canyon echoes speak to a past that still reverberates today? These questions are at the heart of this chapter.

## The Life of Saint George of Choziba

The place to begin is with the story of George, who was abbot of the monastery in the sixth century and for whom the monastery was named. The Life of Saint George of Choziba was written by George's disciple Antony, likely named after the hermit Antony, in the seventh century shortly after George's death. Antony relates the story of George's life and how he came to be the abbot at the monastery in Wadi Qilt. This is not a text with the narrative arc of Athanasius's fourth-century *Life of Antony*, nor does it have the contemplative spirit of some of the sayings of the Desert Fathers. It shares some features with the roughly contemporaneous collection of stories written by John Moschos, *The Spiritual Meadow*: stories of miracles, vignettes of monastic life, insights into the geographical locations of hermitages and monasteries. What's most striking is how the story reveals, through anecdotes and sayings, the geography of the canyon and its reverberant sounds. It is a sensory and sensational story the way Antony tells it. There are other monastic texts that speak to echoes in the desert, but here one gets a clear picture of the sheer canyon walls, precipitous cliff edges, narrow paths in the cliff face, and the reverberance of the canyon itself.

Take, for example, the following brief narrative about George's encounter with a lion just outside the monastery. One day, according to Antony, George went out from the monastery and he

saw a lion lying in front of the doorway. Calmly he nudged the lion with his foot, commanding him to move away from the door so he could leave to take care of his urgent business. But the lion *quietly roared in a friendly way* and wagged his tail that he didn't want to get up. Abba George nudged the lion two or three times with his foot so he would move, but when the lion did not get up, he spoke to him quietly, "Since you do not obey what the scripture says—'The Lord has shattered the lion's teeth; blessed be the Lord' [a

quotation from Psalms 57:7/58:6]—open your mouth
so I can look." The lion opened his large mouth and
allowed him to feel around as much as he wanted.
Then, after he placed his hand in the beast's mouth
and felt around, he said firmly, "Just as a stake in the
wall, a loose one, feels, so too are a lion's incisors!"
Then the lion stood up and went on his way and
George, going out, finished the business he was sup-
posed to do.

Antony here uses the lion quite deliberately to place George
within a biblical and monastic literary tradition and within
a place he seeks to enliven with the sounds of animals and
the sounds of humans. The story of George's encounter with
the lion has many parallels in other monastic texts, including some we have already seen, where injured lions are
healed by monks or roaring lions challenge monks to stay a
solitary course. If we probe the monastic literatures of antiquity, we find that stories of lions played an important role
in the lives of monks. In my view, these stories exceeded
the symbolic realm: lions weren't meant to portray simplis-
tically the dangers of the desert; they also offered monks
an opportunity to reflect on possibilities for human-animal
relationships.

But how does the geography of the canyon come alive in
this text? Another episode reveals more about the canyon
itself:

He lived, [Antony says of George], in a small cell four
to five feet in length, or even much smaller, in which
he recited the divine office in the summer. One night,
then, when it was scorching hot, the enemy of our life
wanted to make him negligent so he would skip the
divine office. Like a huge eagle tall as a man, he stood

on the edge of the roof of the dwelling; spreading his wings, he blocked out the sky. When the old man saw this, he at first marveled at the size of the bird, but then realizing that it was a stratagem of the one who hates what is good, he rushed forward to strike it. But the eagle crashed down the precipice; making a very great noise and crying out with a pitiful screech, with a wail it vanished like smoke.

Here the language of precipices, cliffs, even the implied sense of an abyss create a sense of the striking geography. Likewise, the screech of the eagle, imagined here as a terrifying demon, and its voice crashing down through the canyon adds a sensory detail that would have resonated with monks. The Greek term used here for "crashing" is one we have seen before: *ktupon*—a clashing, thunderous, and dissonant sound. Antony's anecdote about George's hermitage is both evocative and poignant, a place where life is lived on the precipice.

Antony situates George within a monastic tradition and also locates him in Wadi Qilt in the Judean Desert just outside Jerusalem: the language of cells and edges of roofs and precipices paints a portrait of a particular landscape in which both George and Antony reside. The cliffs and the wadi itself, which was also the route to the cells of hermits down the wadi toward the Jordan River, animate a sense of terrain. Perhaps it was the paradoxical precarity and security of canyons that made these places so desirable for monasteries. The canyon paradox, in a sense, compounded the paradox already found in the desert itself, one where the satanic and the sacred were intimately interwoven. The repeated mentions of cliffs and precipices, a trope found in other monastic texts about cliff monasteries, provides a stage for dynamic, sensational, and miraculous stories.

The sounds of animals and the sounds of cliffs are important in the story of George. But so, too, are the stories about human sounds. Once, when some thieves attempted to rob the monastery late one night, "they heard what sounded like a large company of foot soldiers and men on horseback coming towards them" and they ran away terrified. Similarly, George saw a vision on his way to Jericho in which "he heard in the sky a great noise of a crowd of people thrown together against each other, and they were clanging their weapons and crying aloud as though lined up for battle." These stories about military sounds serve as narrative prophecy, for the text also tells about the historical conquest of Persian armies moving toward Jerusalem in the early seventh century.

Throughout the text the sounds of the monks themselves surface in various contexts. The knocking on the monastery's semantron to call monks to prayers, for example, would have echoed through the canyon much like it does today. And Antony writes about "psalms and hymns and spiritual songs" that are offered up by the monks upon George's death. The liturgies the monks now sing at Saint George of Choziba would not have been fully developed in the seventh century, but monks chanting surely reverberated throughout the monastery and the canyon. Acoustical registers of the wadi were punctuated by the sonority of human life at the monastery, and the ambience of late-ancient monastic Wadi Qilt would have been richly varied.

## Travelers' Stories about Wadi Qilt and the Grand Canyon

The acoustical particularities of Wadi Qilt invite comparison to other canyons, and to the cultural impact of canyon sonority more broadly. It may seem odd, perhaps even absurd to compare travelers' representations of Wadi Qilt with those of the Grand Canyon in Arizona. But this comparison illuminates some of the reasons why monks were drawn to canyons of security and danger, silence and sound. The paradoxes were powerful, even seductive.

In John Wesley Powell's famous account of his expedition down the Colorado River in 1869, the Grand Canyon is called "the most sublime spectacle on the earth." He describes "the traveler on the brink [who] looks from afar and is overwhelmed with the sublimity of massive forms; [and] the traveler among the gorges [who] stands in the presence of awful mysteries, profound, solemn, and gloomy." He finds the canyon to be

> the land of music. The river thunders in perpetual roar, swelling in floods of music when the storm gods play upon the rocks and fading away in soft and low murmurs when the infinite blue of heaven is unveiled. With the melody of the great tide rising and falling, swelling and vanishing forever, other melodies are heard in the gorges of the lateral canyons, while the waters plunge in the rapids among the rocks or leap in great cataracts. Thus the Grand Canyon is a land of song. Mountains of music swell in the rivers, hills of music billow in the creeks, and meadows of music murmur in the rills that ripple over the rocks. Altogether it is a symphony of multitudinous melodies.

The Grand Canyon is a geological wonder—277 miles long, in some places 18 miles wide, and a mile deep. Contrasts of mountain and river, sky and rock, and dry heat and cold waters sharpen the senses and fill visitors with awe and fear.

To compare the Grand Canyon to Wadi Qilt, which is a fraction in size and depth, a mere 25 kilometers long, and a few hundred meters deep, may stretch the imagination.

And yet there is a kind of resonance found in late nine-teenth-century surveyors' and travelers' descriptions of Wadi Qilt, revealing shared qualities that transcend the vast dif-ferences in scale. Powell's descriptions of the sublime and gloomy chasm, its noisy and quiet waters, its sheer grandness, the histories written in the rock layers, and the resident in-digenous Indian tribes he encountered reflect an experience of place and geography that can usefully be compared to late nineteenth-century descriptions of Wadi Qilt.

Take, for example, the biblical scholar and ornitholo-gist, Henry Baker Tristram, who traveled to Palestine a de-cade before Powell rafted down the Colorado and de-scribed his experience in Wadi Qilt in his 1865 book *The Land of Israel*:

> And now the scenery changed rapidly to the grand and savage. Instead of limping among the gravels and boulders of winter torrents, with an occasional zizyphus-bush overhanging them, we skirted the tre-mendous gorge of the Wady Kelt, which we could oc-casionally see by peering down the giddy height with its banks fringed by strips of cane and oleander, the "willows by the water-courses." . . . The gorge opens suddenly at a turn of the path about two miles before reaching the plain, where the traveler finds himself in front of a precipice, perhaps 500 feet high, pierced by many inaccessible anchorite caverns, and with a steep, rugged hill above. We gaze down into the steep ravine, and see the ravens, eagles, and griffon-vultures sailing beneath us.

The drama of the wadi, the tensions between "grand" and "savage," hermits' caves along the cliffs, the birds flying below—these descriptions are almost lyrical in their tone.

And yet danger always lurks, toys with travelers' sense of wonder.

J. W. McGarvey, a minister from Lexington, Kentucky, wrote about Wadi Qilt in his 1882 *Lands of the Bible*:

> All is wild and desolate. The road bed has been often shifted by the violence of the winter torrents. . . . When within about three miles of the Jordan Valley you see Wady Kelt, a deep, wild gorge, a short distance to the left; and when within about a quarter of a mile of the valley you pass along the edge of the precipice which forms the southern side of this chasm. It is the darkest and most desolate looking gorge in all Palestine. On either side is a perpendicular wall of dark-brown rock, having a rotten and crumbling appearance, and the narrow bottom of the chasm lies more than 2000 feet below the road. A noisy stream dashes along its rocky bed, distinctly heard on the road above, and a narrow line of verdure marks its course. On one occasion the author entered this gorge at its mouth, where it breaks out into the plain, and ascended it about a mile, partly on horseback and partly on foot. It is scarcely possible to conceive the wild and desolate grandeur of the place. Its brown walls are only about 20 yards apart, and they rise so high and steep as to shut out all the sky, except a narrow strip overhead.

Grandeur, precipitous gorges, wild and desolate and dark, and the constant noise of the water—such images render these gorges and canyons as a kind of otherworldly landscape. And Otherness here reveals both how the sensory landscape affected visitors, how it made them feel, as well as the impact that humans had on the landscape itself. The late nineteenth and early twentieth centuries were an era of exploration and discovery, archaeological excavations and the collection of artifacts, colonial conquest and historical preservation, and in many cases the erasure of one layer of history while protecting another. There are striking parallels between the work of surveyors and explorers in the American West and those in the Middle East/Near East in the nineteenth century. Cumulatively, they offer one angle toward a geocritical understanding of place and how the distinctive acoustic landscapes of canyons, chasms, and gorges— the wadi, nahal, and arroyo—might offer insights into lives lived on the edge, in the abyss, and suspended midway between creek bottoms and a canyon's rim. As the historian Jedediah Rogers has written in his 2013 book *Roads in the Wilderness*, "the landscape of the canyon country has been continually and continues to be created and re-created according to the ideas and values that people bring to it." The deeply evocative structure of canyons, their dark depths and skyward heights, made these places especially potent for lives lived on the fringes of society.

## Life Suspended in Echoes

Stories of cliff monasteries and travelers' impressions of desert canyons draw us toward two striking images. The first is that of echo, one of the most evocative sound-images. The second is that of suspension midway between the sky and the gorge's depths—a kind of halfway point in the middle of grandeur and abyss.

When the *Life of Saint George of Choziba* speaks of the clamor of soldiers and armies, it uses the ancient Greek word, *echo*, from which we derive our own word *echo*. In antiquity, the word could refer to any sound; in the writings of Homer, the word is used for particularly resounding sounds like the noise of a crowd, the roar of a sea, or the groaning of trees in a wind. But it can also refer more specifically to what we think of when we refer to echo: a sound that reverberates against a hard surface and produces what is seemingly an endless fading copy of the initial sound. Our voice speaks back to us in echoing amphitheaters, in hollow canyons, and from rocky cliffsides. Canyons are, after all, a kind of echo chamber. The precise sound of the echo will naturally be shaped by the depth and width of the canyon, by the types of rock and flora on cliff faces, by weather and seasonal changes, and by the varied contours of the rock face.

Wadi Qilt shimmers with reverberance, especially in the area of the Saint George Monastery. But the particular vantage point for listening to echoes significantly affects what one hears. Stand at the bottom of the canyon and the sounds of the stream dominate the soundscape. So, too, birds that gather there in the trees and the wind in the reeds comingle with the water. The echoes rise above you. Hike midway up one of the cliff faces, perhaps to the monastery or to the hermit cave-cells on the north wall, and the sounds of water will lessen, and the sounds of birds now echo around you. At the rim, depending on the season, you might hear just a faint sound of the creek, but the sounds of starlings and ravens echo now beneath you. We have no evidence to suggest that cliff monasteries were built in the middle of canyon walls for that surround-sound experience of echoes, but archaeologists who study cave and canyon acoustics have noted that "echoes can be experienced as voices calling out from the rock." Wadi Qilt, like so many canyons, has a sonority that is especially rich at the midway point.

Stories of cliff monasteries toggle seamlessly between danger and safety of lives lived suspended midway on a cliff. Cliff walls had caves and crevices that were places of safety and solitude, and they were sought by monks precisely for these qualities. Monasteries were built to hang on the cliffs, to merge almost seamlessly with the rock face and to defy architectural logic. But lives clinging to edges were also hazardous and treacherous. Ancient monastic texts speak of the narrow footpaths monks traveled and the danger involved in a simple journey beyond one's hermitage. Life's fragility hung in the balance in these desert canyons in a very real way.

The midway point along a cliff, the middle of a climb, halfway up a canyon's walls—these were poignant and visceral images. In the sixth century, a writer known as Cyril of Scythopolis wrote *Lives of the Monks of Palestine*, an account of the key figures in the history of Palestinian monasticism. One of these figures was the monk Sabas, who, as we have seen, came to live as a hermit in a cave in Wadi Kidron, a canyon located between Bethlehem and the Dead Sea. As a hermit, Sabas attracted many visitors and eventually the most important cliff monastery was built in this canyon to house a growing community of monks. The Mar Saba Monastery is still in use today.

In telling the story of Sabas's cave and the subsequent building of the monastery, Cyril emphasizes the precise location: the cave, he says, was right at the middle point of a cliff face. Cyril describes the difficulties of reaching Sabas's cave and the need for a rope for him to ascend and descend from the cave. Later, as he begins to oversee the construction of the monastery, Cyril writes that "in the middle of the gorge he built a little oratory, in which he set a consecrated altar." The Greek word for "middle" here is *meso*, which meant midway between two locations, in the middle or center of an object or place.

Caves, oratories, and monasteries were suspended in the middle of reverberant canyons. Our word *mediocre* comes from a Latin word that meant "halfway up the mountain." We tend to see mediocre or mediocrity as a failure. To be mediocre is to fail to be excellent, to fail to reach a pinnacle. But monasteries hung halfway in the middle between rim and floor. They were mediocre. I wonder if this linguistic dimension to cliff monastery sites might allow us to recover a sense of perspective that is gained by the midway vantage point. It is from this point we are able to look down into the canyon, sense the dark caverns and lush gardens, and look upward toward the rim, where sky meets the horizon. It is from this point where the sonority of place is perhaps most dynamic. Echoes here may be our own voices returning to us as well as the cacophonies and thrumming of birds, water, wind, sometimes thunder, and clattering rocks.

The phrase "living in an echo chamber" suggests a state of narrow-mindedness and isolation. But the notion of a canyon's echo broadens the perspective. For sure, the sounds monks made by pounding the semantron or walking the canyon trails were reverberant, but so were the sounds of birds and lions and wind. Sound circulates in dynamic cadences through canyons that call us to confront ourselves, our place in these remote locations, and how we respond to the land speaking back to us. We are part of these landscapes: canyons that are constantly changing as rivers continue to carve them, as people move through them, inhabit them, and alter them. As the composer John Luther Adams said about his composition called *The Place Where You Go to Listen*, which he called a "resonating chamber": "Our listening animates the world. And the world listens back."

## CODA

 Desert canyons with the sonorous play of their echoes are deeply evocative places. The monastery of Saint George of Choziba, built into the cliffs of

Wadi Qilt, has its own acoustic signature. On a reverberant spring morning: the dawn chorus of birds, the creek running through pines and palms, the arrival of pilgrims. From the open-air courtyard, we hear the resounding rhythms of the semantron echoing down the gorge. As visitors gather, the monks begin to sing the liturgy in their resonant chapel.

# 6

# ASCENT AT
# SONOROUS SINAI

*going to the mountains is like going home...*
*how truly glorious the landscape circled*
*around this noble summit*
—John Muir, "A Near View of the High Sierra"

I made my first set of desert recordings in the summer of 2012 while traveling with my family in the American Southwest. My goals weren't entirely clear, even to myself, but I knew I wanted to experience listening to the desert and to bring home acoustic snapshots or sound bites that would remind me of the places we visited. At that time, I also wanted to experiment with how listening to the desert today, especially listening deeply through field recording, might help me understand the acoustic registers of the past.

One of the places we visited that summer was the Chiricahua National Monument in the Coronado National Forest of southeast Arizona. The monument is located at the northern end of the Chiricahua Mountains, one of the sky island ranges of southern Arizona, and is reachable by car by way of the Bonita Canyon Drive, which rises from the desert grassland floor of Sulphur Springs Valley. Along the way we watched coati and listened for birds. The terrain changed with our elevation, taking us through riparian woodlands on upward. Massai Point, at 6,600 feet and the end of the drive, is not the highest peak in the Chiricahuas, but the vista is impressive: the view out over the rhyolite spires that dominate the area is otherworldly. Huge rocks, balanced impossibly one on top of another, defy gravity. That summer the scars of wildfires from the previous year—a wildfire known as Horseshoe 2—were dramatic testimony to the transformative power of fire: burnt trees and scalded earth were interspersed with the green and yellow, lichen-covered stone columns.

The hardscrabble landscape matches the heartbreaking history of these mountains, the ancestral homelands of the Chiricahua Apache Indians. In 1886 the Apaches were rounded up and sent to live in Florida; many of them died en route. Massai Point is named for the legendary Chiricahua Apache scout, Massai, also regarded as a "renegade" by late nineteenth-century newspapers, who jumped from the train transporting the Apaches and apparently returned to live on into the early twentieth-century in these mountains. One feels a sense of this storied past, the challenge of life in arid lands, the politics of conquest, violence, destruction, and disenfranchisement. The spires, at least as I regarded them, seemed to witness suffering, standing sentinel and silent.

It was a hot August day with a strong wind, but I still wanted to try to record the ambience of this arid mountaintop. I knew the monastic texts I was studying spoke about wind and fire and mountaintop experiences. The gusting winds made recording difficult, but when I listen to the sounds now here's what I hear: winds that do have a rhythm, winds that howl and gust and hum, and the falling needles of the junipers scattered among the stones and sounding almost like a light rain. The thudding of the wind against the microphones mirrored the wind whipping our ears.

Soon crowds of visitors joined us at the peak. I packed up my recording equipment, and we made our way back down the mountain. In many ways our ascent and descent reverberated with the stories of cliff monasteries, but it also spoke to ancient mountaintop experiences. Several years later, I made recordings at peaks in the Chiricahua Mountains to the south of Massai Point. Here, with elevations of over 8,000 feet, one forgets the hot desert valleys below. It is arid, yes, but the temperature at this height drops, the bird species are different, and the scene is one of coniferous forests, wind in the pines, the clatter of rocks on talus slopes. The place, Barfoot Park and Buena Vista Peak, are a reminder of why mountains have long been considered sacred. Their cool shade and grassy meadows invite rest and contemplation.

Mountains have long been associated with religious life. From its very origins, Christian monasticism went hand in hand with mountain spirituality. Peak experiences were transformational. They are also deeply evocative: the ambient ascent, the noise and silence on thin-aired pinnacles, the throb of one's heart and breath from the climb. Mountains are places to listen.

## Ancient Monasticism and Desert Mountains

Early Christian monasticism built itself onto landscapes that already had long and storied histories. Canyons, wadis, deep ravines—as we saw in the last chapter—were one of these landscapes. Here in the dark depths, monks saw themselves as living in the echo of Elijah and other biblical prophets and they heard the words of the Psalmist, "Yea though I walk in the valley of the shadow of death." Valleys, broad ones like the Zin wilderness we encountered in the first chapter as well as the "gloomy" Wadi Qilt, were potent places that evoked history.

But mountains, a kind of inverted canyon, equally pulled and propelled the early Christian monastic movement. Monasticism was built, in part, from biblical traditions and biblical stories about mountains. Mountains were associated with revelation, transfiguration, and transformation. One of the most important biblical stories for early Christian monks was the story of Moses in the book of Exodus, especially the narratives that associated him with the mountains and wilderness of Egypt and Sinai. He was called by God, Exodus says, while shepherding his flocks in the wilderness near Mount Horeb, also known as Mount Sinai: "There the angel of the Lord appeared to him in a flame of fire out of a bush."

The story of the burning bush, the image of fire, and landscapes of wilderness mountains shaped monasticism in important ways. The story of Moses leading the Israelites out from Egypt through the Red Sea and ascending Mount Sinai to receive the Ten Commandments may well have been the most influential biblical story for monastic practice. It was an ancient story, retold many times by the time that Christian monasticism emerged, and it is a story filled with sound:

On the morning of the third day there was thunder and lightning, as well as a thick cloud on the mountain, and a blast of a trumpet so loud that all the people who were in the camp trembled. Moses brought the people out of the camp to meet God. They took their stand at the foot of the mountain. Now Mount Sinai was wrapped in smoke, because the Lord had descended upon it in fire; the smoke went up like the smoke of a kiln, while the whole mountain shook violently. As the blast of the trumpet grew louder and louder, Moses would speak and God would answer him in thunder. When the Lord descended upon Mount Sinai, to the top of the mountain, the Lord summoned Moses to the top of the mountain, and Moses went up.

This story offers several insights: first, the story depicts a kind of peak experience, a transformative experience, a mountain-top experience. It also speaks to the varied mountain sounds, something John Muir wrote so eloquently about, often with biblical language and metaphors: the voice of God, the blast of the trumpet, the sounds of thunder, the shaking vibrations of the mountain itself. The story inspired listeners with its sensational images.

There is another mountain story from the biblical narratives that comes to reverberate in the early Christian monastic literature—the story of Elijah on, again, Mount Sinai. In the first Book of Kings, the prophet Elijah is called by the "angel of the Lord" to go to "Horeb, the mount of God." When he arrives, he finds a cave and spends the night there. And then God's voice speaks to him:

"Go out and stand on the mountain before the Lord, for the Lord is about to pass by." Now there was a great wind, so strong that it was splitting mountains and breaking rocks in pieces before the Lord, but the Lord was not in the wind; and after the wind an earthquake, but the Lord was not in the earthquake; and after the earthquake a fire, but the Lord was not in the fire; and after the fire a sound of sheer silence.

This story of Elijah's epiphany on Mount Horeb/Mount Sinai shares some of the acoustic elements we find in the story of Moses: wind and earthquakes. And now there is the additional potent "sound of sheer silence." The passage works its drama with stark contrasts: wind, earthquakes, fires; then, utter silence.

These biblical narratives shaped monasticism's relationship to wilderness and, especially, to mountains. Archaeologists of early Christian monasticism have shown the proximity of mountains to the locations for monasteries that were built beginning in the late fourth century. Take the geography of Egypt, for example: the Nile River Valley was (and is) the habitable region, the place where crops could grow and villages flourish. The escarpments on either side, the mountains, were "the desert," the uninhabitable and hostile wilderness. But it is these mountains that drew Christian hermits to their caves and communal monks to build monasteries on their slopes or at their base. It was the mountains in the remote Eastern Desert of Egypt that drew Antony and Paul, where, eventually, in the fifth century monasteries came to be built in their names. In the *Sayings of the Desert Fathers*, monks and pilgrims visit what came to be known as "Antony's mountain," the place of his hermitage and, eventually, his monastery.

So close was the tie between monks and mountains that there is a repeated refrain in the *Sayings*: "If you are a monk, get to the mountain." The languages of Greek and Coptic, which is the latest stage of Egyptian and the language used by Christians in Egypt beginning in the third century, preserve a linguistic connection between monasticism and mountains. In Greek, the word for mountain, *oros*, also came to mean "monastery." Similarly, the Coptic *toou*, "mountain," was used to mean "monastery." So the saying "Get to the mountain" was like saying "Get to the monastery."

Monks were also instructed to be like mountains: "Sing energetically," one of the *Sayings* says, drawing on the words of Psalm 124: "They who have trusted in the Lord are like Mount Zion; he shall never be shaken forever who dwells in Jerusalem." In this passage the mountain where Jerusalem sits, Mount Zion, comes to be a model for how a monk should not be "shaken," not dissuaded from meditation, concentration, and following a monastic path. And stories in John Moschos's *Spiritual Meadow* tell of bright lights shining for days, even months, at the tops of mountains; when people summit the peak to find the source of the light, they find a Christian hermit. Veronica Della Dora, professor of human geography, argued in her 2016 book *Landscape, Nature, and the Sacred in Byzantium* that mountains were "privileged sites for encountering God."

## Monastic Ascent and Descent at Sinai

Among all the mountains mentioned in the monastic literatures, Mount Sinai is the most important, a place of rich resonance and a long history. We have already seen the ancient past of this mountain in the stories of Moses and Elijah. In the Bible, it seems this mountain had two names: Mount Horeb and Mount Sinai. Although historians still debate whether the mountain referred to in the bible is the contemporary granite massif in southern Sinai, we do know that the biblical traditions about Sinai mountains were enormously influential to the development of Christian monasticism. So strong is the traditional association of this mountain with Moses that Muslims continue to call it Jebel Musa in Arabic— Moses's mountain. For thousands of years, this mountain has been considered sacred.

As far as we can tell, Christians began making pilgrimages to Mount Sinai possibly as early as the third century. Over time, hermits came to occupy caves in the mountainous, arid region, and in the sixth century, the Monastery of Saint Catherine was built at the foot of the mountain. This was not the only monastery in the region, but it did come to be the most important and a central focus of pilgrims and monks alike. I last visited this part of southern Sinai and Saint Catherine's Monastery almost forty years ago, and the only sounds I can remember are bellowing camels outside the walls of the monastery, the quiet echoes within the monastery, and the steep quiet ascent in the early hours of the morning to the summit to meet the sunrise. The pinnacle has been experienced by so many people with widely varied stories— of silence, of grandeur, of fear, of exhaustion. Such experiences remind us that there is no single perspective on mountain peaks.

The double meaning of the word *ascent* is especially compelling at Sinai: the rise to a summit and the giving over of one's self to a practice, a discipline, a way of life. The most influential text of Byzantine monasticism, *The Ladder of Divine Ascent*, was written in the seventh century by the abbot of Saint Catherine's Monastery, John Climacus, as previously noted. John's toponymic name *Climacus* comes from the Greek word for "ladder," *climax*, an image bound up with the dual meaning of *ascent*.

We turned to this text in chapter 2 in our inquiry into silence, because this book came to shape the development of hesychasm—the pursuit of inner silence—in later Christian monasticism. But when thinking about peak experiences, it is important to reflect more broadly on how *The Ladder of Divine Ascent* is constructed: as a ladder intended to mirror the climb of a mountain, yes, but also how monastic practice takes practitioners through stages of discipline and contemplation.

*The Ladder* is a complex and long book, but the basic structure rests on the image of a ladder and how the monk can ascend various rungs toward the top of the ladder. Each step is given a theme. The first chapter, the first step, begins with renunciation; here John urges readers to rise above the "noise of the world." We have already seen this idea at the very origin of the hermit's impulse: withdrawal into solitude, silence, stillness. John goes on to speak of climbing the rungs of longing, above all the longing for inner stillness, and he warns readers not to "plunge down the cliffs of despair." Again, the pulls of ascent and descent. In *The Ladder*, we catch a glimpse of how mountains shaped monasticism, textual hints of an ephemeral acoustic past, and the compelling image of peak experience—the ultimate destination of the climb.

One of the striking features of this text is the frequent use of sea metaphors, perhaps in part drawn from the seas on either side of the Sinai Peninsula. In his praise of inner quietude (*hesychia*), John explicitly draws upon these metaphors: "Notice what happens in nature," he says, how "after a storm at sea comes a deep calm." His treatise is meant to help the monk cultivate inner calm in spite of noise, turbulent seas, and distractions. At times, John points the reader towards contemplation by recalling the story of Moses:

> After Moses had seen God in the bush, he went back to Egypt, that is to the darkness and the brick making of Pharaoh who is to be understood here in a spiritual sense. But he returned to the bush. And not only to the bush, but to the mountaintop. For anyone who has experienced contemplation will never despair of himself.

Although the word for contemplation in this passage, *theorema*, carries with it strong visual overtones, it is clear that listening is essential to contemplation for John—listening to silence, inner silence above all, but also to the sounds of wind and water and voice that come to the monk in times of meditation. One of the repeated refrains in *The Ladder* is a quotation from the Gospel of Luke: "He who has ears to hear, let him hear." The monk as listener is key to understanding John's *Ladder*: the monk as listener to scripture, to the "roaring waves of the sea," to the distracting noise of footsteps, to the still small voice of internal quietude. "Ascend, ascend eagerly," John urges his readers at the conclusion of the book. "Let your hearts resolve to climb."

John's *Ladder* is richly resonant with other texts from Sinai from the same time period. The idea of listening—those who have ears to hear should listen—appears in a story told by the seventh-century monk Anastasius of Sinai who, like John Moschos, traveled widely in Sinai and Palestine. In his book called *Tales of the Sinai Fathers*, he writes about services held on the summit of Mount Sinai:

> As the celebrant raised the triumphant hymn, all the mountains responded with an awesome cry, saying three times: "Holy, holy, holy." The cry echoed and lingered for half an hour. This cry was not heard by everyone, but only by those who had those ears about which Christ said: "He who has ears to hear, let him hear."

Even though much in this text is mystical, an ancient sense of listening on mountains and listening to mountains is unmistakable, almost tangible. There is a deep recognition of how hearing might differ from one person to another, how hearing and listening are not the same thing, and how the ability to hear and to listen is shaped not only by our place but also by our intention and our attention.

Sinai is evocative—it calls forth the past, a resonant history, and the paradox of silence and noise—even for those in distant locations. Sinai resounds with history. The art that remains to this day in Saint Catherine's Monastery speaks to the powerful ways in which monks drew upon the images of mountains around them and the rocky landscapes of southern Sinai. And these images transcended the particularities of Sinai itself. As art historians Jas Elsner and Gerhard Wolf write in their essay entitled "The Transfigured Mountain":

> We need to be clear here that Sinaiatic localism, while being specific to the very particular scriptural and liturgical character of the monastery, need not be restricted specifically to that one place. It is a way of being, perhaps even an ideology—or better a spiritual identity—adopted by those (wherever they may be) with a special connection to Sinai.

The idea that the particular—Mount Sinai, Mount Horeb, Jebel Musa—can be translated to other peaks, other places, and other experiences suggests that we have much to learn about listening in mountains. I begin to wonder whether "a way of being," to use Elsner and Worf's phrase, can be found in reverberant and vibrant mountains—a listening way of being.

## Transformative Peak Experiences

In his 2015 book *Landmarks*, Robert Macfarlane writes that "the mountain world, like the desert world, is filled with mirages: tricks of light and perspective, parhelia, fogbows, Brocken spectres, white-outs—illusions brought on by snow, mist, cloud or distance." Macfarlane was drawn to the Cairngorm Mountains of Scotland, in part, by a slim book written during the Second World War by Nan Shepherd, *The Living Mountain*. Not published until 1977, *The Living Mountain* depicts the mountains alive with movement and the ephemeral nature of life. Shepherd writes, "As I penetrate more deeply into the mountain's life, I penetrate also into my own. For an hour I am beyond desire." Even though they write about mountains far from the deserts of the Middle East, Macfarlane and Shepherd speak to something at the heart of the monastic association with mountains: they are places of lore and history, paradoxes of apparent permanence and shifting ephemerality, and above all deeply conflicted human desires.

Mountain lore and the quest for summits are so widespread that we take these impulses for granted. Countless accounts of climbing Mount Everest, with their dramatic and death-defying stories of gear-laden, Sherpa-guided, and oxygen-assisted ascents, have been written. We quest for pinnacles and bag peaks. "*We love the taste of freedom. We enjoy the smell of danger*," wrote Edward Abbey in *Journey Home*, capturing two impulses at work in our drive to summit.

In the monastic context, the image of Moses and Elijah transformed atop a mountain gave the story of a hermit at a pinnacle appearing as a flame or bright light dramatic resonance. And yet monks were wary of euphoria and passion; they worried about emotions and the pride that might come from a peak experience. A mountaintop experience was something to resist as much as it was something to crave.

There is a harsh dissonance between the quest for peak experiences, however, especially those driven by a sense of the sacredness of mountains, and the human hunger for resources that leads to mountaintop removals. Two thousand years ago, Pliny the Elder, in his multivolume work *Natural History*, spoke to mountain mining operations:

A crack gives warning of a crash, and the only person who notices it is the sentinel on the pinnacle of the mountain. He by shout and gesture gives the order for the workmen to be called out and himself at the same moment flies down from his pinnacle. The fractured mountain falls asunder in a wide gap, with a crash which it is impossible for human imagination to conceive, and likewise with an incredibly violent blast of air. The miners gaze as conquerors upon the collapse of Nature.

What Pliny writes about here is what we now call strip mining or mountaintop removal. In our quest for resources—coal, gold, copper—we have stripped bare mountains long considered sacred. Mountains too often lie in ruins in our wake.

In spite of arguments to the contrary, the Bible and the monastic texts are replete with what we might call animism—the sense that the natural world is alive, that it is potent with divine presence, that mountains can burst into song, that they weep and wail with sorrow and shudder with terror. Yes, there is anthropomorphism in these images, and we are wary these days about anthropomorphizing nature. But it is by seeing in nature a reflection of ourselves, and by regarding ourselves as embedded and complicit in the ephemerality of the natural world, that we cultivate empathy for the world we live in. And, in so doing, we may rethink the destruction of mountains, sacred mountains, in our thirst for more.

An excerpt from the Navajo poet Sherwin Bitsui's *Dissolve* speaks profoundly to our intertwined lives with mountains:

This mountain stands near us: *mountaining*,
 it mistakes morning for mourning
 when we wear slippers of steam
  to erase our carbon footprint.

The mountains' fates rest in our hands. And their seeming permanence lies uneasily with our quest for summits. To ascend them requires us to assent to their lessons.

In the late summer of 2019, I visited the Serbian women's Saint Paisius Monastery in Safford, Arizona. Located down a long sandy road in the desert mesquite flatlands of the San Simon Valley, the monastery is easy to miss. Walking the gardens with Sister Nazaria that day, I learned the history of the monastery, which was built on a ranch donated to the sisters by a Christian evangelical family in 1993. Sister Nazaria spoke about how the Apache tribes granted a blessing for the monastery on behalf of Mount Graham, considered sacred by the Apache and located just to the west of the monastery. The story was a vivid reminder of the living relationships between mountains and monasteries.

At Meteora in northern Greece, monasteries are literally grafted onto the tops of mountains, a material echo of the biblical idea of "living stones." Mount Athos, also in Greece, is the center of Greek Orthodox monasticism, and monasteries there were built along sheer cliffs on the mountainous peninsula. At Christ in the Desert monastery in northwestern New Mexico, the sounds of ravens still reverberate off the mountain walls, connecting the monastery to the mountain with sound. The association of ancient monasteries with mountains continues today, resonating with those in the past who made their way in desert mountains, in the winds, noise, and silence of mountaintops, on peaks where transfiguration became visible and sonorous.

## CODA

Mountaintop soundscapes vary from howling and harsh winds to gentle cool breezes. We can track the ascent acoustically by listening to the drone of insects and the calls of doves, quail, and cactus wrens in the desert valley floor, through riparian woodlands with their streams and thrushes, on up through the insects calling on grassy slopes, until we finally reach a cool coniferous forest with its jays and woodpeckers. The clatter of rocks falling on talus slopes reminds us that mountaintops, too, are always changing.

# 7

# FINDING HOME
# IN THE DESERT

Sound is like a warm wind that arises from
my childhood
—N. Scott Momaday, *The Man Made of Words*

There is a day
when the road neither
comes nor goes, and the way
is not a way but a place
—Wendell Berry, "There is a day"

In 2015, my family and I purchased a small off-grid house on seventeen acres in the high desert of remote southeastern Arizona. The round house sits in a valley that doesn't look like much during many parts of the year: at 4,500 feet in elevation, mesquite, creosote, sage, and dusty dirt roads dominate the dry flatlands. Cattle have decimated the once-lush grasslands in this area; dust devils curl through the valley and sandstorms blow in with hot winds. Across the valley to the southeast lie the Peloncillo Mountains of New Mexico. Just beyond the "backyard" of the house, the foothills of the Chiricahua Mountains show the scars of mining still visible on their flanks. The Chiricahua Mountains rise up to almost 10,000 feet, and it is possible to drive from the desert valley through riparian woodlands and on up to a cool coniferous forest in a little over an hour. I love to traverse these micro-habitats more slowly—on foot, remembering that this land is the ancestral home of the Apaches. History is long here, and petroglyphs, grinding stones, and ceramic shards serve as witnesses to the past.

We began going to Arizona every summer beginning in 2010 when our sons were still young. Southeastern Arizona is well known for its biodiversity, situated as it is at the intersection of the Chihuahuan and Sonoran Deserts to the east and west, respectively, and the Sierra Madre Mountains of Mexico and the Mogollon Rim to the south and north. Cave Creek Canyon, at the entrance to the western side of the mountain range, is a beloved birding location; the breeding Elegant Trogon is just one of the attractions in the monsoon season. It's also known for its insects: Vladimir Nabokov used to come to these mountains to collect moths and butterflies. Perhaps surprisingly, August is an especially good time to see wildlife that becomes more active during the monsoon rains. The storms can be quite dramatic: darkening skies, crashing thunder, and torrential downpours. Over the years of living at this house and traveling around the Southwest I have spent many days making field recordings of the desert sounds, especially of wind, thunder, insects, and birds. From beneath the one-seed juniper, with its shaggy flanks where barbed wire from former fence-lines is now embedded, and standing in the shallow arroyo on the property, I watch for and listen to the storms coming from the southwest. The generic and unassuming spot tucked under the tree, neither canyon nor mountain, is as sacred as any I have experienced.

I could not have anticipated how immediate my love for this place would be from the very first time we visited. It was like I had inhaled deep recognition. But quite unlike the deserts of my childhood—the Negev and Sinai Deserts with their barren mountains, the Judean Desert with its folding hills and wadis—the desert landscape in this part of Arizona is rich with vegetation. Only the prickly pear, sage shrubs, junipers, and the occasional acacia tree standing lone in the desert flatlands resonated with my childhood in the Middle East. The ocotillo, agave, and jumping cholla were new cactus species for me to learn, as were the sounds of the cactus wren and roadrunner and many other birds. Of course, the arid air, the need to conserve water, the contentious border issues (the mountains lie just a few dozen miles north of the US-Mexico border), and the historical complexities of conquest and exile resonated with my experiences in Israel-Palestine.

But these days, as I reflect on my sudden affinity for the place and listen to many hours of field recordings I've made in the area, I am struck above all by the cooing of doves, some of the very same species I grew up listening to as a child. Their lilting song evokes my childhood experiences in a very different place. The sounds are, to use the words of N. Scott Momaday in his book *The Man Made of Words*, "like a warm wind that arises from my childhood." It was through listening that I felt on some deep level that I was home, that I had arrived at a place that I recognized and knew in my bones. My own restless personal quest to find home, to find where I belonged, could at last rest. And yet the land's history itself presses against notions of home and belonging, challenging us to rethink "home" altogether. We need to ask what it means to orient ourselves to a place through listening and to engage in a practice of deep listening not only to our own hearts and to our own sense of home but also to other voices, past and present, who have been shaped by acoustical landscapes.

## Monastic Stories of Home

On a fundamental level, monasticism can be understood as intimately tied to concepts and experiences of home. Stories about hermits are about withdrawal, about leaving one's home, family, and friends and traveling to a new place, perhaps a rock-hewn cave, some old ruins, or a monastery at the edge of town or in the remote desert. Monastic texts speak to movement, to migration from one place to another. The stories we have about ancient monks, and modern ones, for that matter, are about leaving home and finding home. Monks lived with a sense of having come from somewhere— the place of childhood, the place of their relatives—and going to a new place, and making that new place home. Some of them came from nearby, like Antony whose home was a village near the Nile. Others came to the deserts of the Middle East from Cyprus, Italy, and Greece. They grafted themselves onto the desert landscapes.

But concepts of "home" in monastic texts are rife with paradox: on the one hand, stories regard a monk's childhood home with family and friends as a burden and a distraction. Family members sometimes pursued their relative-become-monk into the desert, hoping to see their kin. In this sense, one's home never seemed far away. And the monk's desert home was also fraught with new distractions beyond family: demons, wild animals, or pilgrims hoping to see the monk, and the challenges of the communal life in a monastery. A new monastic home was not free of burden, distraction, or danger—quite the opposite. The monastic way was, after all, about the practice of stilling and quieting the inner voices in the midst of outer distractions.

There is another aspect to "home" in monasticism that adds a layer to these paradoxes, for an important theme in these literatures is about whether home is here on earth or home is truly in heaven. There is a decided ambivalence about "home" in the monastic practices of late antiquity. The Greek word *oikos*, "house," could refer to a monk's family home as well as a monk's new dwelling place. And verbal forms of the word—to dwell, to inhabit—are used in multiple ways to describe a monk's dwelling place, the place he or she inhabits, God's dwelling within a monk, and instructions for how monks should dwell with one another. For the monks living in monasteries, dwelling "alone together" was an apt description of the way of life.

The multiple notions of "dwelling" give us insight into practice, but we need to probe more deeply at the paradox of place and, especially, the paradox of home. Home in the desert is sometimes depicted as a kind of paradise in the stories of monks. Antony's story is an excellent example of this phenomenon. In Athanasius's story, Antony's final stage of withdrawal and migration was necessary because the desert around Antony became a city of monks. Countless visitors traveled to see him, to ask him for healing, and to imitate him. Over time, Antony again heard a call to withdraw (*anachoresis*) and to go to "the interior desert" for solitude. In response to this call, Antony migrated to a place near Mount Kolzim, as far as we can tell—the mountain in the eastern desert of Egypt where, eventually, a monastery came to be built in his name that still stands today.

The story of him finding this place, his place, is in many ways the climax of the narrative, even though it appears in the middle of Athanasius's story. The passage, a biblical echo, says that Antony traveled for "three days and three nights" to come to a high mountain, where

at the foot of the mountain was a spring with very clear water, sweet and very cold. Some ways from the mountain was a plain, and a few untended date palms. Antony,

> as someone moved by God, loved the place, for this
> was the place indicated by the voice that spoke to him
> on the riverbank. . . . He was like someone who rec-
> ognizes his own home: from that point on he consid-
> ered the place his own.

Antony at last found home. It was a place of some beauty in
Athanasius's rendering; with its clear sweet water and date
palms, it was the perfect place for the way of solitude, for the
pursuit of a holy loneliness. In Athanasius's dramatic and
sensational story of Antony, this passage strikes me as an
emotional, even tender moment about finding home, finding the place where one belongs. Antony was moved, he
loved the place, and he regarded it as his own.

Writing just a few decades after Athanasius, Jerome writes
a similar story about a certain Paul, whom he calls "the first
hermit." Paul, like Antony, journeyed into the desert and at
last he found, Jerome says:

> a rocky mountain, at the foot of which, closed by a
> stone, was a cave of no great size. He removed the stone
> (so eager are men to learn what is hidden), made eager
> search, and saw within a large hall, open to the sky,
> but shaded by the wide-spread branches of an ancient
> palm. The tree, however, did not conceal a fountain
> of transparent clearness, the waters whereof no sooner
> gushed forth than the stream was swallowed up in a small
> opening of the same ground which gave it birth. . . .
> Accordingly, regarding his abode as a gift from God, he
> fell in love with it, and there in prayer and solitude
> spent all the rest of his life.

This passage echoes the story of Antony and adds the cave
within which is a palm tree and gushing stream. Like Antony, Paul "fell in love with it." Jerome writes in Latin, and

the word he uses here for "love" is *adamato*, coming from the Latin verb *adamo*, which meant "to love truly, earnestly, and deeply." What's striking about Jerome's choice of word here is that it would have resonated for him and his readers with the very word he used in his Latin translation of the Bible. There, *adamo* referred to what we would call "romantic love" or "falling in love"—the love and desire of one person for another.

The stories of Antony and Paul falling in love with their desert homes may, on one level, be understood as a literary trope: a departure, a quest, the finding of home—a home in the desert that is beautiful and beckons us toward it. A story recounted by an anchorite in Sinai repeats the image of "this cave, this spring, and that palm tree" as all that was necessary for a hermitage, a home. In this sense there is something in these stories that echoes the ancient pastoral literary traditions of wilderness but also gestures forward in time toward romantic ideas. Romanticism, the cultural geographer Yi-Fu Tuan reminds us in his 2013 book *Romantic Geography*, "inclines toward extremes in feeling, imagining, and thinking." Tuan also notes how "quest is at the heart of romance," and here, I think, lies one of the important features of the stories of Antony, Paul, and other ancient monks: quests driven by longing, arrivals found by a sense of recognition. Here is Tuan again: "'Home' is for the far-ranging human mind." The monastic stories describe the marriage of an earthly place—the spring at the base of the mountain for Antony, the cave with a palm and gushing stream for Paul—with an imagined paradise. In this way, there is a kind of resolution to the tensions between earthly and heavenly homes.

Historian Virginia Burrus, in her 2019 book *Ancient Christian Ecopoetics*, identifies the stories of Antony and Paul as part of a literary tradition about a "happy place" (in Latin, *locus amoenus*). The stories of Antony and Paul finding their "happy place" are not unique: the sixth-century female ascetic in the Judean Desert Syncletica, too, was reported to have said: "God led me to this place and when I saw this cave I entered it with joy." But Burrus reminds us that this "happy place" is not unambivalent. These stories of hermits are set in desert places that are both a refuge and danger, a solace and treacherous. This is, in part, the lesson of the desert—a place of powerful paradox. But it is also a commentary on the paradox of home.

## At Home in the Desert

What does it mean to find joy in a desert place, to fall in love with a cave, a spring, a single palm tree? Is it desperation born of a fraught life? Discipline of religious zeal? An ancient quest to downsize and simplify? The stories about Antony, Paul, and Syncletica's love for a desert place echo in the twentieth-century writings of Mary Austin and Edward Abbey. With Austin and Abbey, we flesh out the human quest for home and that sense of recognizing a place where you feel you belong. A feeling of home might take time to develop, while in other cases it seems nearly instantaneous.

In her 1932 memoir, *Earth Horizon*, naturalist, conservationist, and poet Mary Austin wrote about leaving her home in Illinois to homestead with her family in the Tejon region of the San Joaquin Valley of California. Much of her memoir is written in the third person. Here is a passage about her arrival by train in California: "All that long stretch between Salt Lake and Sacramento Pass, the realization of presence which the desert was ever after to have for her, grew upon her mind; not the warm tingling presence of wooded hills and winding creeks, but something brooding and aloof, charged with a dire indifference, of which she was never for an instant afraid." Austin's use of the word "presence" here highlights the pull of the desert on her imagination and experience. And yet her description of the desert as "brooding and aloof" is hardly a phrase we would associate with attraction. It is the "indifference" of the desert that most seems to draw her.

Eventually, Austin moved to the southern end of the San Joaquin Valley and into the Mojave Desert, where she wrote her most well-known book, *The Land of Little Rain*, in 1903. Her love for the desert is palpable in this book, which reverberates with biblical echoes and the stories of ancient Christian monks. It is difficult not to read her praise of the desert as a kind of romantic theology: "There is the divinest," she writes, "cleanest air to be breathed anywhere in God's world"; "deep breaths, deep sleep, and the communion of stars"; "the silence of great space." *The Land of Little Rain* romanticizes the desert and sees it for what it is—challenging, "a lonely land" where "you cannot go so far that life and death are not before you."

The novelist and environmental writer Edward Abbey wrote in his 1977 memoir, *The Journey Home*, about his own arrival in the "Great American Desert" from his home in Pennsylvania:

> In my case it was love at first sight. This desert, all deserts, any desert. No matter where my head and feet may go, my heart and my entrails stay behind, here on the clean, true, comfortable rock, under the black sun of God's forsaken country. When I take on my next incarnation, my bones will remain bleaching nicely in a stone gulch under the rim of some faraway plateau, way out there in the back of beyond.

For all of his disavowal of religion, Abbey's writings about the desert are deeply imbued with biblical language and sublime praise. Unlike Austin, who encouraged people to come to the desert and stay, Abbey's goal was to keep people out.

As part of the early stages of the environmental movement, Abbey was a fierce advocate for conservation. But the tension remains: with their sensational descriptions and lively stories, his books inspired many people to come to the deserts of Utah where he worked as a National Park Service ranger in Arches National Park for several seasons.

The stories and writings of Austin and Abbey, like the stories of monks, are more than just stories about a double life, a before and after, a here and there. They are more than stories about finding home. They also speak to movements and migrations that grew themselves into, or grafted themselves onto, a desert landscape, one that had already been inhabited for centuries. In some cases the ruins of past lives became the home of present lives. At other times, their arrival required the active removal of those who lived there. Newcomers made these places "their own," oftentimes by imagining a desert that was empty, uninhabited, and by reshaping the desert landscape. And this draws us into the politics of home, the politics of not only emplacement, being in place, but also displacement.

Rosemary Marangoly George, the late professor of English literature, wrote in her 1996 book *The Politics of Home* about how "home is a way of establishing difference." This compelling point offers a nuanced understanding of home that goes far beyond the place where we live. Monks were drawn to the idea and the reality of the desert because it was different; it was set apart from village and city life, and the monks sought solitude, silence, difference. In this sense, the ancient definition of "sacred" also seems particularly fitting—a place set apart, consecrated, different. And by "finding home," the monks made the unfamiliar, the different, home.

Austin and Abbey, too, were drawn to the desert because something in its difference spoke to them. Thoreau asked in his book *The Maine Woods*, "*Who* are we? *Where* are we?" In raising such questions, he points to how our identities are tied to place. And this is what is at stake in finding home—our very sense of self. Such a quest necessarily involves difference. In his epilogue to the 2006 *The New Desert Reader*, Peter Wild reflects on the tensions between the emotional and romantic view of the desert and the scientific work of preserving the desert, between what he calls "fantasy and reality." But these "contradictions," he writes, "challenge us to become more aware both of ourselves and of the desert's complexities."

The questions around our identification with place, whether it is the place where we grew up or a place that somehow (inexplicably?) attracts us, are not easy to resolve. Who owns a place? Who gets to call a place home? In what ways do our views on home harmonize with our views of belonging and in what ways might they stand in tension with one another? And, as we think about listening, we should ask: How do the sounds of a place affectively attract us? What do they make us feel, remember, and think? Listening, after all, might lead us back to a deep sense of belonging that transcends place.

## The Sounds of Home

Midway through the spring of 2020, my university closed because of the COVID-19 pandemic and my students were sent home or to their apartments off campus. In the midst of the abrupt closure, I asked students (now via Zoom) in my "Sound, Silence, and the Sacred" seminar, who had been making recordings each week during the semester, to record the sounds of home or to record how sounds may have been changed with the shutdown, the "New York pause," or the shelter-in-place orders. Half of the students noticed that the loudest sounds they now experienced were the sounds of cooking, their mother's voice, their own soft humming while they studied. They noticed how the sound of their dishwasher was a signature sound of home. The other half, going outside, remarked that the loudest sounds were the springtime songs of birds. The world around them had become empty and silent: roads normally loud with trucks and cars went quiet; the din of campus life had ended; and even the skies were emptied of the sounds of jets. Their papers noted just how much the sounds of home set them in a place, a place of memory and belonging, if now an uneasy and strange one.

In her 2016 article "Aural Postcards," Fran Tonkiss writes about the "souveniring" of sounds, about collecting sounds from different places one travels. In some ways, this is what I was asking my students to do by recording sounds each week—to treat them as souvenirs of time and place. My own first impulses toward field recording were similar. But there is something more to it, because "sound," as Tonkiss continues, "threads itself through the memory of place." For listeners, sounds enliven and deepen the experience of home and of places that captivate inner longings. Sound, as I have been suggesting in this book, is a primary way in which we experience place. The sounds of a new place can be terrifying and may take time to become familiar. On the other hand, the familiar sounds of home can trigger memories, nostalgia, fear, or longing.

In the story of Paul finding home in a cave with a spring, readers are asked to imagine the sound of the stream that gushes from within the cave, a desert place with plentiful waters. Antony's sweet spring likewise encourages not only a sense of taste, but also hearing and listening. Austin and Abbey's experience of the desert was deeply shaped by sound: their writings tune our ears to the sounds of wind and water, the sounds of thunder and birds and coyotes. Austin describes, for example, the "three kinds of noises buzzards make"; how "the desert spring is voiced by the mourning doves"; and the "thunder of falls, wind in the pine leaves, or rush and roar of rain."

Finding home by way of sound, through listening to sound, is not exclusive to humans. Scientists have learned the countless ways in which the animal (and plant) worlds use sound and hearing to orient themselves. They teach us how to become better listeners. We have long known that bats use echolocation: they emit clicks from their mouths that echo against objects in their surroundings in order to avoid obstacles as they fly and find prey. Whales tune themselves to their pods, calling to one another, as a way of orienting themselves. Homing pigeons may well use their acute sense of hearing as a way to return home. And in one of the incredible feats of the animal world, the migration of birds, we are beginning to learn more about how birds fly thousands of miles to return home and the role that sound might play in finding the same place each year.

When I first began experimenting with field recordings, I often made them with my sons in tow. I listen back now to those recordings and I hear their young voices, high pitched and excited. These sounds are intimately tied to my sense of home. One of the reasons that "home" may be so fraught is that it speaks to who we are, our sense of selves, where we came from and who we become. My recordings return me to a time and place, a memory of tender, if also exhausting and frustrating, days. Even in a desert, I couldn't find quiet! And how our voices changed the soundscape of the desert!

As we listen for our place in the world, it may be that we have more questions than answers. What memories of home are made vivid through sound? Does listening cultivate a sense of recognition or alienation? And what causes us to recognize, sometimes instantaneously, the sense of belonging in a place? The pull of attraction and attachment takes us back and forward in time. For deep listeners these pulls are shaped by the sonorous and the sensuous. Can an *acoustic ecology of belonging* tend and cultivate an inclusive way to listen deeply in the present and to the past, to the ways in which sounds shape our inner sense of self and the sound-scapes around us? Might the sounds of a place, flowing in and around a place and intermingling with other sounds, teach us about what it means to belong?

The phenomenon of sound and the sense of belonging are both fluid, ever ephemeral, always changing. Sounds sound in our world and then they dissipate; our attachments to place change over the course of our lives. These two ever-shifting spheres inform one another profoundly, and they help us attend not only to memory and longing, but to the present ephemeral moment.

## CODA

What does home sound like? How do we recognize home by listening? For each of us, the answers will be different. When I hear pigeons and doves at a desert spring, or the chatter of sparrows in a single acacia tree, I am reminded of my childhood. These days, home means standing on a remote gravel road listening to thunder across the desert valley, the songs of birds in the late afternoon, and the calls of crickets as night winds move through juniper, sage, and cactus.

# EPILOGUE

I could not have anticipated how the themes of this book—sound, solitude, silence, nature, and home—would take on new meaning in the late stages of my writing. When the COVID-19 pandemic began to spread in the spring of 2020, I was working to revise chapters. Our lives were upended, disrupted. Our world did not look the same and it did not sound the same. On a global, unprecedented scale, we were required to stay home, shelter in place, isolate. The idea of staying safe by staying home, however, is not at all simple. For many, home is actually a place where the threat of violence is omnipresent, and studies showed that domestic abuse rose significantly during the lockdowns. The paradox of home as refuge and danger surfaced in urgent ways as we were told to stay home.

So, too, the politics of home emerged during the pandemic when the homeless who sleep in subways and migrants and refugees searching for safety were forced into closely confined tents and makeshift buildings. We don't yet seem to be able to confront on a national scale, let alone a global scale, what home might mean as we still face a pandemic and hopefully emerge from it. Can we reimagine how we belong to place? How we might live in harmony with place? How place can be transformed by our behavior? And how we cultivate an environment where all flourish? These questions are now all the more pressing.

As I finished revisions from my home in rural central New York during March of 2020, every weekday sounded like a Sunday—the day when traffic on the two-lane highway, located just half a mile from my house and heading into the town of Ithaca, is drastically reduced. A day of quiet. That spring, public and private schools, colleges, and universities closed their doors and sent students home; restaurants and bars and gyms shut their doors; public transportation largely ceased running; nonessential businesses closed; the local quarry turned off the conveyer belts and stone crushers. No trucks, no airplanes, no cars. Everyone was told to lock down and self-isolate. In striking ways, our world went eerily silent: less traffic, fewer planes, a Sunday stillness every day. My neighbors and I noticed this quiet. And folks around the world noticed the unsettling silence, a stillness in cities and countryside as the world faced a pandemic together. Social media channels were alive with details (and recordings) of the altered soundscapes. So much of the monastic idea of silence and noise, as well as solitude and community—the alone togetherness—now became vivid in a new and dramatic way.

At the same time, it was March and the snow had largely melted, the light was returning. Much of our acoustic world was just ramping up and tuning its rich vocal chords. The red-wing blackbirds returned and they perched around the pond rasping across their acoustic territories and waiting for the females to arrive; the song sparrows and Carolina wrens and chickadees whistled in the shrubs; the relentlessly shrill peepers began calls, and then the wood frogs chimed in with their low clucking. All was a chorus out there in the natural world. It was hardly silent. We heard an amplification, in fact, of the seasonal and migrational changes to our sounding world. Normally, the sounds of traffic would detract from my enjoyment of the spring sounds, and normally the silencing of traffic would be welcome to my ears. That particular spring, though, was hardly normal and the silence was a bit eerie. I tried to savor the sonority and the opportunity to listen to the sounds of nature that are often obscured by our own din. And I reflected on my changing relationship to silence. I developed a practice of sitting in a forest glen each morning, listening to the ambient world.

In the din of our urban and busy lives, silent retreats may be welcome and savored. But when we need to quarantine, silence may become, as the saying goes, deafening. The lockdown gave me time to reconsider my own conflicted relationship with silence. In some ways, I set out years ago to understand early Christian monasticism and to practice field recording as a way to find silence. I hoped to experience quiet stillness by making field recordings in the remotest desert locations I could find—to mimic the monks of antiquity who sought the desert for solitude and silence. But I found instead just how much I live ambivalently in relationship to silence. I crave quiet. I find that the noise of the world—highways that are ever expanding, air traffic, sounds of children, even those children we love—makes me long for quieter places. And yet silence can also be a punishment. One monastic saying resonates deeply and troublingly with my own childhood: "Speak if you are asked; otherwise, keep silent." Silence speaks now to isolation and social distancing in new ways. Yet it also resonates with the ambivalence of ancient monks about silence and solitude. I kept asking myself: In the midst of a pandemic, can we think of silence not so much as absence, but rather as the full presence of quiet—a rare opportunity to slow down, recover a place where we might dwell, perhaps briefly, in contemplative attention?

 Again the desert and its sounds can teach us. The desert only *seems* deserted. It only *seems* silent. It only *seems* to be a place for solitude. It only *seems* to be permanent. In the ever-shifting desert hills, canyons, mountains, and ephemeral streams, we find evocative lessons for listening and for being present in the world. The parched landscape reveals, perhaps surprisingly, the fullness of life; the apparent emptiness helps us embrace community; the bareness cultivates a rich experience. The echoes ricocheting against rocky escarpments and in dark caves remind us that we are joined to those of the past, those who heard and watched, feared and hoped, those whose voices still speak across time and place. If only we pause to listen deeply.

# Acknowledgments

My profound gratitude goes out to so many who have helped me bring this book and these recordings into the world: to nature guides in the Negev and Texas deserts, to the monks and nuns who offered me hospitality, to my hosts in disparate places, to photography teachers and friends, to sound artists and field recordists, to listeners, desert lovers, and fellow seekers I've met along the way, to audiences at numerous academic institutions around the world, and to colleagues, friends, and students, who have offered encouragement, countless conversations, and generous insights.

There are too many individuals who have contributed to this project to list by name, but I want to single out a few in particular: warmest thanks to Darlene Brooks Hedstrom, who first suggested that I make my experiences recording in the desert integral to the story; to Chrysi Kotsifou, who transformed a field recording trip to Wadi Qilt and Deir Hajla into a profound once-in-a-lifetime experience; to Georgia Frank, Carrie Koplinka-Loehr, and Matthew Westermayer, who read the full manuscript and gently corrected and queried me about my ideas and my writing; and to Bill McQuay, who took my raw footage and created audio montages that allowed me to express and share the lively sonority of deserts with readers and listeners.

I'm grateful, too, for the fellowships, grants, and awards I've received in support of my research: in particular, the American Academy of Religion, Cornell University's Atkinson Center for a Sustainable Future and the Society for the Humanities, the Mellon Foundation, and the Op-Ed Project.

Resounding thanks to Cornell's Bioacoustics Research Program and the Macaulay Library of Natural Sounds, especially Greg Budney, the former curator of the Macaulay Library, and Bill McQuay, audio producer and sound engineer, and current founder and head of Eco Location Sound: The Art of Sound Informed by Science (https://ecolocationsound .com/).

I could not have written this book without the extraordinary writing coach, teacher, and publishing expert, co-founder of She Writes Press, Brooke Warner, who challenged me to work and rework my chaotic research and writing about deserts, sound, and monasticism; helped me create a whole story from disparate parts; encouraged me to find my north star and my voice; and buoyed me up when I thought I might not find readers and fellow listeners. Deep thanks and deep bows to you, Brooke.

And then there is what I call my "dream team": the editors, design and marketing experts, audio engineers, everyone at Princeton University Press who has made it possible for me to share my stories with the world. I am profoundly grateful to my editor and publisher, Fred Appel, who believed in this book, patiently asked about it every now and then, and then showered me with enthusiasm in the final stages; and to digital and audio publisher Kimberley Williams. What a joy, a dream, to work with everyone at PUP to see this book through to the finish line and beyond.

Last and most of all, I want to thank my family: my parents for giving me a most sonorous childhood, one made for listening; my sister and brother who shared that childhood with me. And all my love and gratitude to John, Eli, and Ben who have shared this book's journey with me from its beginning: to my husband John, who built me a writing studio where it is quiet and I can be alone, helped me purchase our off-grid happy-place desert home, generously provided his own professional recording and audio editing expertise, and above all continues to share this listening life with me; and to our sons, Eli and Ben, whose passion for the natural world inspires me to be hopeful and to savor every wondrous encounter with rattlesnakes and turtles, coatimundi and javelinas, trogons and ravens. You have my heart, forever and always.

# Desert Monasticism:
## A Brief Glossary

Anchorite: Comes from the Greek verb ἀναχωρέω (*anachoreo*) which means to "retire, withdraw" (i.e., withdraw from battle, leave a place) and the noun ἀναχώρησις (*anachoresis*), which means "place of retirement, refuge, retreat." It comes to mean the same thing as *hermit*: "one who lives in solitude," in contrast to the *cenobite*, who lives in community.

Asceticism: Comes from the Greek noun ἄσκησις (*askesis*), which means "exercise, practice, training; way of life." We use this term now in English to refer to a wide array of practices that discipline the body and deny pleasure, such as becoming a monk or nun and vowing celibacy, taking up the life of a hermit, or even practices of long fasting. The range of practices can be quite wide.

Cenobite: This word derives from a combination of the Greek nouns κοινωνία (*koinonia*), which means "association, partnership, fellowship" and βίος (*bios*), which means "life." In the New Testament, the word *koinonia* refers to close relationships or participation/sharing in something, such as sharing in the presence of the Holy Spirit. The Greek words came to be combined in late Latin as *coenobita*, which referred to a person who becomes a monk in a communal monastery, and *coenobium*, the monastery itself.

Desert: Comes from the Latin noun *desertus*, which means "deserted, free of people, uninhabited; a wilderness; lonely, solitary." Although deserts are often identified by their low rates of precipitation, it's more accurate to identify them as regions where the amount of moisture lost into the atmosphere (through, for example, evaporation) is greater than the amount of rain received. Deserts are tremendously varied and exist on all continents, including the polar regions.

Hermit: This word comes from two closely related Greek words, the noun ἐρημία (*eremia*), which means "solitude, desert, wilderness; state of loneliness or solitude," and the adjective ἔρημος (*eremos*), which means "desolate, lone, lonely, lonesome, solitary; unfrequented, abandoned, deserted." The adjective is also used as a noun, and then it means "desert, wilderness." The uncommon but useful English words *eremite* ("hermit") or *eremitical* ("living as a hermit") come from these Greek words.

Hesychasm: Perhaps more than any of the other terms in this glossary, this word has complexity and long-lasting historical influence. The word comes from the Greek word ἡσυχία (hesychia), which meant "solitude, silence, quietude, stillness, rest." It is such a multivalent word that it becomes difficult to translate in English. But it is essential for understanding the monastic traditions of the East, especially for the development of thought and practice that sought to understand the relationship between inner and outer silence.

Monasticism: The term comes from the Greek adjective μοναχός (monachos), which means "single, solitary." This is not a word that appears in the New Testament at all, but sometime in the fourth century the Greek word came to mean "monk." We use monasticism to refer quite broadly to the many varieties of practices of asceticism and prayer, including communal monasteries and/or hermitages in urban and/or remote settings. In terms of world religions, Christianity and Buddhism have the most developed traditions of monasticism.

# A Guide to Monastic Texts

This is a brief chronological guide to the main monastic texts I discuss in the book. It is intended to help readers find readily available English translations of these texts, which are a fraction of the monastic literatures written during the fourth through seventh centuries and beyond. Many of these texts are also available online now in digital collections of early Christian and medieval texts. For published works, the primary presses for Christian monastic texts are Paulist Press, especially in their Classics of Western Spirituality series; Saint Vladimir's Seminary Press, based in Crestwood, New York; and Cistercian Publications, whose editorial offices are at the Abbey of Gethsemani in Kentucky, and which is now affiliated with Liturgical Press in Collegeville, Minnesota. For those wanting bibliographic information as well as a survey of the history of monasticism in its first few centuries, I recommend William Harmless, *An Introduction to the Literature of Early Monasticism* (New York: Oxford University Press, 2004).

### Athanasius, *Life of Antony* (fourth century)

Two English translations are readily available. I recommend especially the translation done by Tim Vivian and Apostolos N. Athanassakis, *The Life of Antony by Athanasius of Alexandria* (Kalamazoo, MI: Cistercian Publications, 2003a). This translation is based on the best edition of the Greek and Coptic versions of the *Life of Antony,* and the translators provide English translations of both versions, so readers can compare how the *Life* in Coptic differed from the *Life* in Greek. There is also an earlier translation, done by Robert C. Gregg, *Athanasius: The Life of Antony and the Letter to Marcellinus* (New York: Paulist Press, 1980). Both of these published translations also offer rich introductions to the history of Athanasius and Antony.

### Jerome, *Life of Paul, the First Hermit* (fourth century)

Translations of Jerome's *Life of Paul,* which tells not only the story of Paul but also how Antony traveled to find Paul in the desert, are available in multiple editions. For ease, the translation done by Caroline White, *Early Christian Lives* (Penguin Classics, 1998) is a good place to begin. The advantage of this book is that in addition to Jerome's *Life of Paul* it also contains a translation of Athanasius's *Life of Antony* as well as Jerome's

*Life of Hilarion* and *Life of Malchus*, the *Life of Martin* written by Sulpicius Severus in the fifth century, and the *Life of Benedict* written by Pope Gregory I in the sixth century.

### Sayings of the Desert Fathers (fifth century)

As I mention in chapter 1, this anonymously written collection of sayings and stories of monks has a complex history, in part because it probably began as an oral collection—stories that circulated among monks and their visitors in Egypt and then Palestine. It also circulated in two versions: one organized thematically and the other organized by names of monks. The newest translation of the thematic version of the *Sayings* is by John Wortley, *The Book of the Elders: Sayings of the Desert Fathers* (Collegeville, MN: Liturgical Press; Cistercian Publications number 240, 2012). An earlier translation by Benedicta Ward, *The Sayings of the Desert Fathers: The Alphabetical Collection* (Kalamazoo, MI: Cistercian Publications, 1975), translates the alphabetical version based on the names of monks.

### Histories of the Monks of Egypt (likely early fifth century)

This is an anonymous history of the monks of Egypt, organized by the names of the monks. This collection of stories, like Palladius's collection below, with which it sometimes overlaps, contains short vignettes from their lives. Norman Russell has translated the Latin version under the title *The Lives of the Desert Fathers* (Kalamazoo, MI: Cistercian Publications, 1980). I also discuss in chapter 3 a story that comes from the earlier writings of Paphnutius (fourth century) called *Histories of the Monks of Upper Egypt*. This work has been translated by Tim Vivian as *Histories of the Monks of Upper Egypt and the Life of Onnophrius* (Kalamazoo, MI: Cistercian Publications, 1993).

### Palladius, Lausiac History (fifth century)

Palladius traveled from Asia Minor (modern-day Turkey) to visit the monks of Egypt, and he wound up staying for a decade or so. He wrote *Lausiac History* as a record or memoir of his time in Egypt. As with the anonymous collections, this text is a combination of sayings and short stories or anecdotes about the monks. It is available in a translation by John Wortley, *The Lausiac History* (Collegeville, MN: Liturgical Press; Cistercian publications, vol. 252, 2015).

### Besa, Life of Shenoute (late fifth century)

Shenoute was abbot of the White Monastery in Upper Egypt during the fifth century. His *Life* was written by his successor at the monastery, Besa, who wrote in Coptic, just as Shenoute had. A translation of this *Life of Shenoute* has been done by David N. Bell, *The Life of Shenoute* (Kalamazoo, MI: Cistercian Publications, 1983).

### Cyril of Scythopolis, *The Lives of the Monks of Palestine* (sixth century)

Cyril was a monk from Scythopolis in Palestine (modern-day Bet Shean in the southern part of the Galilee region in northern Israel). He traveled to Jerusalem and then on to the monasteries of the Judean desert, especially learning from Sabas. His *Lives of the Monks of Palestine* contains a lengthy introductory section that outlines the history of monasticism in Palestine; then he turns to lengthier stories, including the lives of Euthymius, Sabas, John the Hesychast, Cyriacus Theodosius, Theognius, and Abraamius. An English translation was done by John Binns, *Lives of the Monks of Palestine by Cyril of Scythopolis* (Kalamazoo, MI: Cistercian Publications, 1991).

### John Moschos, *The Spiritual Meadow* (early seventh century)

As far as we can tell, John came from Damascus, Syria, and traveled throughout Palestine and Egypt collecting stories of monks during the sixth century. The text is organized very simply around these short stories, or vignettes, and along the way we gain insights into monasticism during the time as well as political changes taking place in the region. I recommend the English translation by John Wortley, *The Spiritual Meadow (Pratum Spirituale)* (Kalamazoo, MI: Cistercian Publications, 1992).

### Antony, *Life of Saint George of Choziba* (seventh century)

As I discuss in chapter 5, this text offers telling insights into the geography of Judean Desert cliff monasticism, especially the monastery of Saint George of Choziba. The most accessible English translation is one done by Tim Vivian (along with Apostolos N. Athanassakis): Tim Vivian, *Journeying into God: Seven Early Monastic Lives* (Minneapolis, MN: Fortress Press, 1996). This volume also contains translations of the stories of a monk named Pambo and the nun Syncletica of Palestine, as well as the *Life of Abba Aaron*. Vivian's introduction to the *Life of Saint George of Choziba* is especially rich with information about the geography, daily life, and history of the monastery.

### John Climacus, *Ladder of Divine Ascent* (seventh century)

John was a hermit for most of his monastic life, but eventually he came to lead the Monastery of Saint Catherine in Sinai. His treatise, *Ladder of Divine Ascent*, became an essential text for Byzantine monasticism. There is an English translation done by Colm Luibheid and Norman Russell, *John Climacus: The Ladder of Divine Ascent* (New York: Paulist Press 1982), which also contains a lengthy introduction written by Kallistos Ware.

### Anastasius of Sinai, *Tales of the Sinai Fathers* (late seventh century)

There is much we do not know about the writer Anastasius and about the history of this book, but his *Tales* are part of a larger corpus of writings from Sinai and offer important insights into the history of monasticism in Sinai. Here I recommend Daniel F. Caner, *History and Hagiography from the Late Antique Sinai* (Liverpool: Liverpool University Press, 2010), which includes selections from other writers about monasticism in Sinai that serve as a rich supplement to John Climacus.

# Notes

## Epigraph

vii     "Listening is a primary mode": John Luther Adams, *The Place Where You Go to Listen* (Middletown, CT: Wesleyan University Press, 2009), p. 104.

## Chapter One: Listening to the Desert

1     "world is made of sound": Tommy Orange, *There, There: A Novel* (New York: Alfred A. Knopf, 2019), p. 210.

1     "every soul has a distinct song": Joy Harjo, *Crazy Brave: A Memoir* (New York: W. W. Norton & Company, 2012), p. 19.

5     "Egypt's deserts were the edge of the world": William Harmless, *Desert Christians: An Introduction to the Literature of Early Monasticism* (New York: Oxford University Press, 2004), p. 3.

7     "listen with the ear of the heart": Benedict of Nursia, *Monastic Rule*, preface. For details on the publications of monastic sources, see the Monastic Sources Reading Guide.

9     "there is a common misconception that deaf people live in a world of silence": Evelyn Glennie, "Hearing Essay," available online at https://www.evelyn.co.uk/hearing-essay/ (accessed August 9, 2020).

10     "submerged in sound and vibration": Michael Stocker, *Hear Where We Are: Sound, Ecology, and Sense of Place* (New York: Springer, 2013), p. 2.

10     "the body is that mysterious": David Abram, *The Spell of the Sensuous* (New York: Vintage Books, 1996), p. 37.

10–11     "over increasingly large areas": Rachel Carson, *Silent Spring* (Boston: Houghton Mifflin, 1962), p. 103.

11     "we set out to tame the rivers": Marc Reisner, *Cadillac Desert: The American West and Its Disappearing Water* (New York: Penguin, 1987), p. 486.

11     "dry places": William deBuys, *A Great Aridness: Climate Change and the Future of the American Southwest* (New York: Oxford University Press, 2011), p. 10.

12     "sounds like a train coming too fast around a curve": Norman Maclean, *Young Men and Fire* (Chicago and London: The University of Chicago Press, 2017 [c. 1992]), p. 41.

13     "Christianity is the most anthropocentric": Lynn White Jr., "The Historical Roots of Our Ecological Crisis," in *Science* 155 (March 10, 1967: pp. 1203–7); reprinted in *The Ecocriticism Reader: Landmarks in Literary Ecology*, ed. Cheryll Glotfelty and Harold Fromm (Athens and London: University of Georgia Press, 1996), p. 9.

15     "sheer silence": 1 Kings 19:12.

15     "no sound is heard in the desert": Eucherius, *In Praise of the Desert* 37, translated by Tim Vivian, Kim Vivian, and Jeffrey Burton Russell, *The Lives of the Jura Fathers: The Life and Rule of the Holy Fathers Romanus, Lupicinus, and Eugendus, Abbots of the Monasteries in the Jura Mountains* (Kalamazoo, MI: Cistercian Publications, 1999), p. 211.

15     "friendly silence of the desert" and "silence" that torments: T. E. Lawrence, *Seven Pillars of Wisdom* (New York: Doubleday, 1935), pp. 548 and 85.

15     "the desert is overwhelmingly silent": John C. Van Dyke, *The Desert* (New York: Scribner, 1908), p. 27.

16     "howling wilderness": Deuteronomy 32:10.

16     "noise of the falling water": C. Leonard Woolley and T. E. Lawrence, *The Wilderness of Zin*, originally published in the *Palestine Exploration Fund Annual* 1914–1915; reprinted edition (Winona Lake, IN: Eisenbrauns, 2003), p. 27.

17     "an arid zone": Nick Middleton, *Deserts: A Very Short Introduction* (New York: Oxford University Press, 2009), p. 3.

19     "the souvenir speaks": Susan Stewart, *On Longing: Narratives of the Miniature, the Gigantic, the Souvenir, the Collection* (Durham and London: Duke University Press, 1993), p. 135.

20     "if you're a field recordist": Peter Cusack, interviewed by Cathy Lane, in Cathy Lane and Angus Carlyle, *In the Field: The Art of Field Recording* (Devon: Uniformbooks, 2013), p. 192.

## Chapter Two: Hermits and the Quest for Solitude

23     "what draws us into the desert": Edward Abbey, *A Voice Crying in the Wilderness (Vox Clamantis in Deserto): Notes from a Secret Journal* (New York: St. Martin's Press, 1989), p. 85.

23     "there is no possible return": Edmond Jabès, *Intimations The Desert*, translated by Rosmarie Waldrop, *From the Book to the Book: An Edmond Jabès Reader* (Hanover and London: Wesleyan University Press, 1991), p. 166.

23 "the creek that actually burbles": Jim Harrison, "Sky," from his collection of poems *Songs of Unreason* (Port Townsend, WA: Copper Canyon Press, 2011), p. 83.

26 "unaffected by the outside world": Athanasius, *Life of Antony* 1.3. See "A Guide to Monastic Texts" in this book.

27 "do not be concerned about tomorrow": Gospel of Matthew 6:34.

28 "helps in forcing a breakthrough": Belden C. Lane, *The Solace of Fierce Landscapes: Exploring Desert and Mountain Spirituality* (New York: Oxford University Press, 1998), p. 39.

28 "in front of his house" and "no monk knew": *Life of Antony* 3.1.

29 "the Christian monk was formed": David Brakke, *Demons and the Making of the Monk: Spiritual Combat in Early Christianity* (Cambridge, MA: Harvard University Press, 2006), p. 5.

30 "the demons made such a racket": *Life of Antony* 9.5–7.

31 "what sounded like mobs": *Life of Antony* 13.1.

31 "the desert was made a city": *Life of Antony* 14.7.

31 "frequently, without becoming visible" and "they do all these things": *Life of Antony* 25–26.

33 "fled to the mountain wilds": Jerome, *Life of Paul the First Hermit* 5. See "A Guide to Monastic Texts" in this book.

33 "make it your home": Cyril of Scythopolis, *The Life of Sabas* 15. See "A Guide to Monastic Texts."

34 "solitude was not merely an escape": Peter France, *Hermits: The Insights of Solitude* (New York: St. Martin's Press, 1996), p. 26.

36 "Why do I live alone?": from Thomas Merton, *Learning to Love: Exploring Solitude and Freedom* (San Francisco: Harper, 1997), p. 342.

38 "Let the place of the solitaires": from *Wallace Stevens: The Collected Poems* (New York: Vintage, 1990). [In the public domain.]

## Chapter Three: A Way of Silence in a Noisy World

41 "Instead of raw or achieved silence": Susan Sontag, "Aesthetics of Silence," in her *Styles of Radical Will* (New York: Picador, 2002), p. 10.

41 "works to protect": from the National Park's Natural Sound and Night Skies website, https://www.nps.gov/orgs/1050/whatwedo.htm (accessed August 5, 2020).

44 "out of primitive stillness": Hillel Schwartz, *Making Noise: From Babel to the Big Bang and Beyond* (New York: Zone Books, 2011), p. 20.

44 "darkness and silence were before": Pseudo-Philo 60:2 as translated by D. J. Harrington in *The Old Testament Pseudepigrapha*, vol. 2, ed. James H. Charlesworth (New York: Doubleday, 1985).

44      "for many millions of years": Mike Goldsmith, *Discord: The Story of Noise* (New York: Oxford University Press, 2012), p. 17.

45      "silence is an invention": Ilya Kaminsky, *Deaf Republic: Poems* (Minneapolis: Graywolf Press, 2019), notes.

47      "silence . . . is the dimension": N. Scott Momaday, *The Man Made of Words: Essays, Stories, Passages* (New York: St. Martin's Griffin, 1997), p. 16.

47      "huge dogs": John Moschos, *The Spiritual Meadow*, supplemental tales, Nissen 6. See "A Guide to Monastic Texts."

49      "such was his silence": *The Book of the Elders: Sayings of the Desert Fathers* 18.45. See "A Guide to Monastic Texts."

50      "the ones who pray to God": *The Book of the Elders: Sayings of the Desert Fathers* 12.25.

51      "An elder said, 'In the same way'": *The Book of the Elders: Sayings of the Desert Fathers* 2.33.

51      "*Hesychia* is a key word": in Kallistos Ware's introduction to *John Climacus: The Ladder of Divine Ascent*, translated by Colm Luibheid and Norman Russell (Mahwah, NJ: Paulist Press, 1982), p. 50.

52      "the beginning of *hesychia*": John Climacus, *Ladder of Divine Ascent* 27.402. See "A Guide to Monastic Texts."

52      "he who has achieved *hesychia*": John Climacus, *Ladder of Divine Ascent* 22.405–6.

53      "the effect of the sun on the stones": Thomas Merton, "Love for God and Mutual Charity," Thomas Merton's lectures on hesychasm to the novices at the Abbey of Gethsemani, transcribed and edited by Bernadette Dieker; published in *Merton and Hesychasm: The Prayer of the Heart*, edited by Bernadette Dieker and Jonathan Montaldo (Louisville, KY: Fons Vitai, 2003), p. 462.

54      "by keeping even one square inch": Gordon Hempton, *One Square Inch of Silence: One Man's Search for Silence in a Noisy World* (New York: Free Press, 2009), p. 16.

54–55      "In America, there is no monastic foundation" and "a monastery is not a refuge": the quotations by Thomas Merton and Aelred Wall are found, respectively, in a brochure distributed by the monastery and in Mari Graña, *Brothers of the Desert: The Story of the Monastery of Christ in the Desert* (Santa Fe, NM: Sunstone Press, 2006), p. 13.

56      "Whether we see silence as the way": Sara Maitland, *A Book of Silence* (Berkeley: Counterpoint, 2008), p. 279.

## Chapter Four: Monastic Desert Soundscapes

59 "Now I will do nothing but listen": Walt Whitman, "Song of Myself" section 26 found in *Walt Whitman: The Complete Poems*, edited by Francis Murphy (London: Penguin, 2004).

60 "noiselessly": Robert T. Hill, "Running the Cañons of the Rio Grande," excerpts taken from *God's Country or Devil's Playground: The Best Nature Writing from the Big Bend of Texas*, edited by Barney Nelson (Austin: University of Texas Press, 2002), pp. 7–26.

61 "obliterate every sign": interview with Julia Nail Moss can be found at https://scholarworks.utep.edu/interviews/864/ (accessed September 15, 2021).

62 "Today all sounds belong": R. Murray Schafer, *The Soundscape: Our Sonic Environment and the Tuning of the World* (Rochester, VT: Destiny Books, 1994; originally published New York: Knopf, 1977), p. 5.

63 "the study of the effects": Barry Truax, editor, *Handbook for Acoustic Ecology* (Vancouver: A.R.C. Publications, 1978; see also the 1999 CD-ROM version).

63 "all sounds, those of biophony": Bryan C. Pijanowski et al, "Soundscape Ecology: The Science of Sound in the Landscape," *Bioscience* 61.3 (March 2011): p. 204.

64–65 "each story is based on listening": Donald Kroodsma, *The Singing Life of Birds* (Boston and New York: Houghton Mifflin, 2005), p. x.

66–67 "whether there came a whistling wind": *Wisdom of Solomon* 17:18–21. This text can be found in any Bible that includes the Apocrypha. The translation here is taken from *The New Oxford Annotated Study Bible*, Fully Revised Fifth Edition (New York: Oxford University Press, 2018).

68 "moving air": Lyall Watson, *Heaven's Breath: A Natural History of the Wind* (New York: NYRB Classics, 2019).

68 "One day Abba Arsenius": *The Book of the Elders, Sayings of the Desert Fathers* 2.25.

68–69 "the huge rocks lying in the water": Paphnutius, *Histories of the Monks of Upper Egypt* 2.27. See "A Guide to Monastic Texts."

70 "do not again put it in your heart": Besa, *The Life of Shenoute* 151–53. Translated by David N. Bell (Kalamazoo, MI: Cistercian Publications 1983).

70 "ravens that permits": Bernd Heinrich, *Mind of the Raven: Investigations and Adventures with Wolf-Birds* (New York: Harper Collins, 1999), p. 31.

71 "in order to assure that an increasing population": The Wilderness Act, available online at https://www.fsa.usda.gov/Assets

/USDA-FSA-Public/usdafiles/Environ-Cultural/wilderness
_act.pdf (accessed August 10, 2020).

72    "sense of nature as a picturesque commodity": Alison Byerly, "The
      Uses of Landscape: The Picturesque Aesthetic and the National
      Park System," in *The Ecocriticism Reader* (see above), p. 59.

72    "It has always been part of basic human experience": Gary Snyder,
      *The Practice of the Wild* (Berkeley, CA: Counterpoint, 1990), p. 7.

## Chapter Five: Echoes in Sacred Canyons

75      "the remembered canyon silence": Wallace Stegner, *The Sound
        of Mountain Water* (Lincoln and London: University of Nebraska
        Press, 1985; copyright 1965), p. 132.

80–81   "saw a lion lying": *Life of Saint George of Choziba* 2.10. See "A
        Guide to Monastic Texts."

81–82   "He lived in a small cell": *Life of Saint George of Choziba* 3.13.

83      "they heard what sounded" and "he heard in the sky": *Life of
        Saint George of Choziba* 6.28 and 7.30.

84      "the most sublime spectacle" and "the traveler on the brink" and
        "the land of music": John Wesley Powell, *The Exploration of the
        Colorado River and Its Canyons* (New York: Penguin, 1987; copy-
        right 1875), pp. 390, 389, and 394, respectively.

85      "And now the scenery changed": Henry Baker Tristram, *The
        Land of Israel: A Journal of Travels in Palestine, Undertaken with
        Special Reference to Its Physical Character* (London: Society for
        Promoting Christian Knowledge, 1865), pp. 199–200.

86      "All is wild and desolate": J. W. McGarvey, *Lands of the Bible: A
        Geographical and Topographical Description of Palestine, with Let-
        ters of Travel in Egypt, Syria, Asia Minor, and Greece* (Philadel-
        phia: J. B. Lippincott, 1882), p. 234.

87      "the landscape of the canyon country": Jedediah S. Rogers,
        *Roads in the Willderness: Conflict in Canyon Country* (Salt Lake
        City: University of Utah Press, 2013), p. 166.

88      "echoes can be experienced as voices": Steven J. Waller, "Inten-
        tionality of Rock-Art Placement Deduced from Acoustical Mea-
        surements and Echo Myths," in *Archaeoacoustics*, edited by Chris
        Scarre and Graeme Lawson (Cambridge: McDonald Institute for
        Archaeological Research, 2006), p. 35.

89      "in the middle of the gorge": *Life of Sabas* 16.

90      "our listening animates": John Luther Adams, *The Place Where
        You Go to Listen* (Middletown, CT: Wesleyan University Press,
        2009), p. 104.

## Chapter Six: Ascent at Sonorous Sinai

93      "going to the mountains": John Muir, "A Near View of the High Sierra," in *Essential Muir*, edited by Fred D. White (Berkeley: Heyday and Santa Clara University, 2006), pp. 45 and 48.

96      "there the angel of the Lord": Exodus 3:2.

96–97      "On the morning of the third day": Exodus 19:16–20.

97      "Go out and stand": 1 Kings 19:11–12.

99      "privileged sites for encountering": Veronica Della Dora, *Landscape, Nature, and the Sacred in Byzantium* (Cambridge: Cambridge University Press, 2016), p. 148.

101      "After Moses had seen God": *Ladder of Divine Ascent* 5.780.

102      "as the celebrant raised": Anastasius of Sinai, *Tales of the Sinai Fathers* 1.6. See "A Guide to Monastic Texts."

103      "We need to be clear here": Jas Elsner and Gerhard Wolf, "The Transfigured Mountain: Icons and Transformations of Pilgrimage at the Monastery of St Catherine at Mount Sinai," in *Approaching the Holy Mountain: Art and Liturgy at St Catherine's Monastery in the Sinai* (Belgium: Brepols, 2010), p. 42.

103      "the mountain world": Robert Macfarlane, *Landmarks* (London: Penguin, 2015), p. 67.

103–4      "as I penetrate more deeply": Nan Shepherd, *The Living Mountain* (Edinburgh and London: Canongate, 2011; first published in 1977), p. 108.

104      "We love the taste of freedom": Edward Abbey, *Journey Home: Some Words in Defense of the American West* (New York: E. P. Dutton, 1977), p. 215.

104–5      "A crack gives warning of a crash": Pliny the Elder, *Natural History* (Loeb Classical Library; Cambridge, MA: Harvard University Press, 1952), 33.21.

105      "This mountain stands near us": from Sherwin Bitsui, *Dissolve* (Port Townsend, WA: Copper Canyon Press, 2019), p. 16.

## Chapter Seven: Finding Home in the Desert

109      "sound is like a warm wind": N. Scott Momaday, *The Man Made of Words: Essays, Stories, Passages* (New York: St. Martin's Griffin, 1997), p. 7.

109      "there is a day": Wendell Berry, *A Timbered Choir: The Sabbath Poems 1979–1997* (New York: Counterpoint, 1998), p. 216. Credit: Wendell Berry, ["There is a day"] from *This Day: Collected and New Sabbath Poems 1979–2012*. Copyright © 2013

by Wendell Berry. Reprinted with the permission of The Permissions Company, LLC on behalf of Counterpoint Press, counterpointpress.com.

113–14     "at the foot of the mountain": *Life of Antony* 49–50.

114     "a rocky mountain": *Life of Paul* 5–6.

115     "inclines towards extremes in feeling" and "quest is at the heart": Yi-Fu Tuan, *Romantic Geography: In Search of the Sublime Landscape* (Madison: University of Wisconsin Press, 2013), p. 6 and 27.

115     "'home' is for the far-ranging": Yi-Fu Tuan, *Romantic Geography*, p. 177.

115     "happy place": Virginia Burrus, *Ancient Christian Ecopoetics: Cosmologies, Saints, Things* (Philadelphia: University of Pennsylvania Press, 2019), p. 99.

116     "All that long stretch": Mary Austin, *Earth Horizon: Autobiography* (Boston and New York: Houghton Mifflin, 1932), p. 182.

117     "In my case it was love": Edward Abbey, *The Journey Home: Some Words in Defense of the American West* (New York: E. P. Dutton, 1977), p. 12.

118     "home is a way": Rosemary Marangoly George, *The Politics of Home: Postcolonial Relocations and Twentieth-Century Fiction* (Berkeley: University of California Press, 1999), p. 2.

118     "*Who* are we?": Henry David Thoreau, *The Maine Woods* (available now online at: https://www.gutenberg.org/cache/epub /42500/pg42500-images.html; accessed September 15, 2021).

119     "challenge us to become": Peter Wild, *The New Desert Reader: Descriptions of America's Arid Regions* (Salt Lake City: The University of Utah Press, 2006), p. 306.

120     "threads itself through the memory": Fran Tonkiss, "Aural Postcards: Sound, Memory and the City," in *The Auditory Culture Reader* (London; Bloomsbury, 2016), p. 245.

120–21     "three kinds of noises" and other quotations: Mary Austin, *The Land of Little Rain*, pp. 21, 36, 58.

# Photographs

Fig. 1    My recording equipment in the Negev's Zin Wilderness, Israel

Fig. 2    Hermitage in Wadi Qilt, Judean Desert, Israel

Fig. 3    Titus Canyon, Death Valley National Park, California

Fig. 4    Pecos River, Texas

Fig. 5    Monastery of Saint George of Choziba, Wadi Qilt, Judean
          Desert, Israel

Fig. 6    Chiricahua Mountains, southeastern Arizona

Fig. 7    Rain shower in the Chiricahua Mountains, Arizona

# Recording Locations
# for Chapter Codas

Chapter 1    Listening to the Desert: Negev Desert

Chapter 2    Hermits and the Quest for Solitude: southwestern Texas

Chapter 3    A Way of Silence in a Noisy World: Mojave Desert, southern
             California; northwestern New Mexico; southeastern Arizona

Chapter 4    Monastic Desert Soundscapes: southern Nevada; southeastern
             Arizona; Mojave Desert, southern California

Chapter 5    Echoes in Sacred Canyons: Wadi Qilt, Judean Desert

Chapter 6    Ascent at Sonorous Sinai: southeastern Arizona

Chapter 7    Finding Home in the Desert: Negev Desert; southeastern
             Arizona

Printed in the USA
CPSIA information can be obtained
at www.ICGtesting.com
JSHW030922080324
58776JS00005B/7